MANAGING GROUP TOURS

Your Complete Reference Guide
To Successful Tour Management

by
Anita L. Fielder

Tour Management
Your Complete Reference Guide to Successful Tour Management

New Revised Edition, Copyright ©1995
by Anita L. Fielder

Shoreline Creations, Ltd.
143 Douglas, Suite 8
Holland, Michigan 49424
(616) 393-2077
(616) 393-0085 fax

Notice of Liability:
This publication is designed to provide accurate and authoritative information with regard to the subject matter covered. It is sold with the understanding that the publisher is not engaged in rendering legal, accounting, or other professional advice. If legal advice or other expert professional assistance is required, the services of a competent professional person should be sought.
From "Declaration of Principles" jointly adopted by a Committee of the American Bar Association and a Committee of Publishers and Associations.

Library of Congress Catalog Card No.: 95-67422

ISBN 1-887067-51-5

Publisher: Carl Wassink, Shoreline Creations, Ltd.
Editor: Amber Christman-Clark, Shoreline Creations, Ltd.
Designer: Amy E. Gustin, Shoreline Creations, Ltd.

Printed in Grand Rapids, Michigan

Acknowledgments

The origin of this book began many years ago with the frequent questions of my friends and tour members. Many of them had become intrigued with the tour business and thought they would like to be involved. Some of them were interested in occasional while others sought to establish tour programs of their own.

I completed the first book, *Tour Management*, in an effort to answer those inquiries. It soon found its way to travel schools, colleges and universities who were earnestly seeking resources for their tour management courses. Their request for a textbook on the subject, led to a revision of the first book into a new and more comprehensive version entitled *Managing Group Tours*.

We hope that this publication will be a useful and inspiring resource for students in the travel curriculum. This book would not have become a reality without the encouragement and help of Carl Wassink and the staff of Shoreline Creations. Thanks also for the editing assistance of Amber Christman-Clark and Judy Barnes. My sincere appreciation goes to Amy Gustin, Mary Hames and Beverly Hoover for their helpful design efforts, as well as the technical assistance of Randee Bowlin. I have learned much from the many colleagues and travel co-workers who shared in this fascinating business. Silent partners in this effort have been the hundreds of tour members who shared the travel miles and made them into great tour experiences.

As always, my sincere thanks to my friends and family for their continued support and enthusiasm for my writing endeavors.

Anita Fielder

Contents

Preface

Chances are that you, like many people, have considered a career in the travel industry. Very likely, the kind of job you find most appealing is in the area of group tour management. We all are fascinated with the opportunity to travel world-wide and we believe that to pursue it professionally would be ideal.

But organizing and directing group tours is a complex and challenging effort. It requires:

- a thorough knowledge of the travel industry and how it functions
- an understanding of the group tour business as a vital segment of the travel industry
- well developed abilities to organize and manage tour plans and procedures
- the ability to locate and use information that is current and useful in management decisions
- responsible business practices

Unlike many kinds of jobs, tour management does not make allowances for the beginner's lack of experience. It requires that every trip is conscientiously planned to protect the safety, well-being and satisfactions of people who have placed their trust in the tour company. No single tour can afford to gamble on luck or "get-by" arrangements because it involves important responsibilities. Whether your group is a small, informal club on a brief get-a-way jaunt or an international tour for hundreds, the responsibilities are equally important.

Managing Group Tours was written to help you as an aspiring tour manager. Hopefully, the information provided will start you on your way to effective planning, marketing, and guiding your tours. Your future in this field of work can bring you many satisfactions and the chance to advance to even more exciting challenges.

TRAVEL & TOURISM IN THE 1990s

CHAPTER ONE

And now, finally, there is some good news!

Economists are predicting that recovery is in sight for American businesses. After the past five or six years of disabling financial stress, even a moderate growth in profits is encouraging.

The recession was first felt in the late 1980s by oil companies and major manufacturers. Gradually, it moved from the coastal cities to involve the entire nation and all income levels. Alarmed investors saw their profits dwindle and massive layoffs meant unemployment in many industries. Soon, consumers began to limit their spending to necessities with an eye on the dollar value of every purchase. Some skeptics warned that the travel and tourism industries would face disastrous results. And it did leave some serious scars, but in the final analysis, travel/tourism proved to be one of the healthiest survivors of the financial crises.

Transportation, especially the airlines, suffered the early impact of the downturn. The high cost of operating their schedules drove a number of airlines to seek bankruptcy protection, but they coped and found ways to keep their

Affects On The Travel Industry

prices at an affordable level for the public. They had to reduce the numbers of flights, arrange "no-frills" schedules, and set up mergers with regional airlines to retain their service to outlying areas. Soon they were announcing discounted fares and special promotions, which of course prompted their competitors to do the same, producing fare wars. At a time when they had planned to add aircraft to their fleet, their focus instead had to be on maintenance, security and retaining a loyal satisfied public.

The same kind of shock waves spread to the hotel industry, cruise lines, resorts and theme parks. Some of the "status" hotel systems developed or acquired moderately priced hotel chains to retain their volume of customers. Many linked up with popular attractions, so they could lure new economy-minded clients. When the financial stress was greatest, some were rescued by foreign investors from Japan and European economies.

But they made it, and now these same businesses are already announcing plans for growth and expansion. Throughout the entire uncertain period, all of these companies continued intense and effective marketing programs. They handled the crisis and still kept the public eager and willing to travel.

Travel/Tourism... Healthy Survivors

To the surprise of skeptics, fewer than 5% of the travel agencies closed their businesses. In fact, 1993 figures of overall profits in travel income showed a modest 3% gain, and the predictions for the coming years are even more encouraging.

There is also good news for people who are involved in the tourism segment of the travel occupations. Group travel has proven to be the strongest and most durable part of the business. Certainly, consumers became more cautious about spending their limited dollars on vacation trips, but they have also discovered that group tours are a wise value choice.

Undoubtedly, they have learned the many genuine advantages of well-planned group tours.

Travel - An Unusual Profession

Let's consider the ways that the travel industry is unique - unlike most other businesses. In general, business firms deal in the marketing of products and services. Their major efforts are focused on providing a product(s) or service(s) for the consumer. To ensure sales, they promote a demand for the product through advertising and other creative marketing methods. If the buying public ceases to demand the product or services, the firm either creates another saleable item or adapts the ones they have. Otherwise their business is in trouble.

The travel/tourism industries are also selling services. Here, their function is one of reserving and selling the services of other businesses. It might be a steamship cruise, an airline flight or lodging in a hotel—any number of travelers' needs. All of these services are provided by other firms (suppliers) with the travel agency or tour manager serving as the arranger, coordinator and business transactor. The remarkable part of this system is that the service of the travel agency is provided to the customer (client) usually at no charge. Instead, the travel firm receives a commission from the suppliers whose services are sold. This is the source of income for the agency.

Indirectly, a part of every travel reservation/sale is returned to the agency. Commissions vary widely —from 7% to 15% or more — with most of the suppliers offering 10% to 12% commissions. Therefore, bookkeeping and accounting are extremely important in the travel business.

In many ways, it seems surprising that travel could have developed into such a sound and enduring system. In only a half century, it has become a remarkable giant in the business world, with billions of dollars in transactions. It has accom-

The main function of the travel/tourism industry to reserve and sell the services of other businesses.

plished all of this through effective organization and careful attention to details. All of this was done for millions of clients who, one by one, requested and received the services that filled their particular needs. This surely is custom-selling at its best.

Survival Factors for Travel/Tourism

One of the main reasons that the business has endured is the flexibility with which it can function. Although these firms have well established long range plans, their operations are specifically organized into travel seasons. This is a real advantage, because they can adapt each season's offerings to be in tune with special conditions and events of interest.

Some of these are one-time events, but significant enough to justify the effort for the thousands of people who will be interested to attend. Consider recent examples such as:

The tour planner can adapt each season's offerings to be in tune with special conditions and events of interest.

- The 50th anniversary of D-Day in Normandy
- World Cup Soccer Championship games
- Olympic competitions and Goodwill games

You might think that travel planners are at a severe disadvantage since they must depend on the availability of suppliers. At a time when a depressed economy might cause several suppliers to fold their businesses, it could spell disaster for the planner. Fortunately, competition brings in a good variety of suppliers for them to draw on. Nearly every destination has multiple suppliers who are eager and ready to book arrangements. For popular trips, there can be an access of five or six airlines, a dozen different hotels and many restaurants — plenty from which to choose.

Of course, the travel agent or tour planner needs information about those availabilities and the quality of their services. Most agencies have computerized information at their fingertips, so they can be easily informed about services to recommend.

Continued Strong Demand

The main reason that the travel business has survived so well is that travel needs have become a part of our lives. Fast, safe, and convenient transportation has helped us to shape our lives and to become what we are — as a nation and part of the global community. It has expanded and strengthened our business and professional opportunities and enriched our personal lives. The public has become so dependent on travel services that we simply would not know how to function without them.

Corporate Travel

No one depends more heavily on travel than the men and women of the business world. Once, corporations were limited to the state or region where they were located for most of their functioning. Now their executives can easily operate branch divisions in Seattle, Toronto, Tokyo, or even Cairo. Their sales representatives are no longer restricted to local regions of operation. Thousands of business persons follow schedules that routinely take them from San Diego on Tuesday to Wilmington by Thursday. Extensive travel demands of this type are so common that some of the large firms have needed to establish their own corporate travel divisions within the company. Most, however, contract their business accounts through large travel agencies.

Suppliers also recognize the benefits gained from corporate travel. Airports, hotels, and resorts have made all kinds of adaptations in schedules and facilities to make them more convenient and receptive to business needs. Whether it is inflight phones, or special office work areas with computer, fax, and secretarial services, these amenities have simplified business travel and eased the stresses involved.

Travel has always been a part of the professional person's game plan. It has made possible an education in a distant prestigious college or university. It provides opportunities for contacts with leaders in their field through seminars,

> **No one depends more heavily on travel than the men and women of the business world.**

conferences and even research projects they may be pursuing. Being able to travel may have made some of the best parts of their careers possible.

Governmental Operations

Probably no segment of our society has grown to depend more on travel for accomplishing their purposes than government employees. Aspiring candidates chalk up millions of miles on their campaign trails. Even more jaunts are involved as legislators commute to and from their cities of operation. If we consider the special tours of negotiating teams for national and international diplomacy, then add on all of the support personnel and media involved in these events, astronomical totals appear.

Much official travel is provided by government and military transportation, but most is in the hands of the travel industry. Travel makes it possible to operate our governmental programs and functions in the world community — even to wage war or to ensure peace —halfway around the globe.

Personal Travel

The most rapidly growing segment of the travel market is the general public. These are the customers who choose to travel for their own special purposes and satisfactions. They have learned that their trips can be pleasant and enrich their lives in many ways. Now they can:

- Find a relaxing escape from the increasing frenzy of their pressured lives.
- Maintain their bonds with personal and family contacts who have rapidly scattered to many places throughout the country.
- Visit the spectacular and scenic sites that had formerly seemed as impossible dreams.
- Pursue adventures to give their lives new dimensions.

Probably no segment of our society has grown to depend more on travel for accomplishing their purposes than government employees

- Learn about other countries, cultures and significant historical events.

The enthusiasm of the public hasn't faded, even with the limited funds that a recession may bring. Our pleasure-oriented society still places travel high on their priority lists. Travel firms, including suppliers of all types have become sensitive to these economic pressures and have produced some remarkably creative plans to keep America traveling.

Our pleasure-oriented society still places travel high on their priority lists.

Response to Social Trends

The past decade will go down in history as a period of unprecedented rapid social change. These are trends that are shown in our lifestyles, attitudes and relationships. Travel/tourism is closely involved in people's lives, so it is forced to acknowledge these trends. When we realize the priorities that exist in the minds of the buying public, we can shape our services to satisfy their goals. Travel suppliers are extremely alert to the strong motivations of the public. For example:

- Environmental concerns
- Health and security precautions
- Accessibility by handicapped persons

Social trends extend far beyond to recreation, the arts and family life, however. It is interesting to see how current enthusiasm for country/western trends in music, folk arts, festivals and even theme parks has grown. The success of Nashville and Branson has spread to many states, to the profit and delight of enthusiastic developers.

Close on the heels of every recession comes the "quick-rich" schemes and gambling casinos. A few years ago, there were only a few states where gambling was legal — and relatively few race tracks. No longer limited to Las Vegas or Atlantic City, fortune seekers can now find casinos in 37

**Travel suppliers
are extremely
alert to the strong
motivations
of the public.**

states. Opportunities exist from Deadwood, S.D., to New Orleans, La., as well as riverboats along the Mississippi or on any sizable lake and on many Indian Reservations–where ever they may choose. In fact, gambling and race track tours are among the most popular trips these days.

Amusement parks and resorts frequently publicize their additional timely features each year, for example Lion King Country and White Water Rafting Adventures. It's all a part of creative marketing and travel suppliers are experts in capitalizing on such trends. They keep a close watch on general social trends, too. With the continuing emphasis on family values, we see more services that cater to the needs of the modern family. There are special family cruises, kids free programs, single parent vacations, and grandparent/grand-child promotions, just to list a few. Actually, the new pressures of this forced adaptability may have brought about some needed innovations. To that end it is particularly helpful to the industry.

Challenges in the 1990's

There are some trends in this decade that present some serious concerns to travel/tourism. No survey of the field would be valid without recognizing them.

Travel has a great blending effect on groups of people. Tourists from all economic, ethnic and cultural levels come together — so do their activities, attitudes and misbehaviors. Reports of crime and violence (major and minor) in many locations have sent a message of caution and anxiety for many travelers. Warnings about security and safety are not conducive to a tourist's peace of mind. Travel managers cannot ignore this very real problem, but must keep it in perspective in all of their planning and promotion.

Planners who are involved in international tours may be especially concerned and check regularly with the published lists of restricted destinations. Many months of advanced planning are necessary for some of the tours and conditions are not always predictable.

Most problems and concerns can be averted or anticipated, but some appear with little or no warning. These are times that challenge the real strength and adaptability of a travel firm. The past months and years have brought an unprecedented series of natural disasters: earthquakes, fires, floods, hurricanes and a record setting winter of bitterly cold, snowy weather across the United States. Travel depends upon advanced planning and lead time, and unexpected conditions call for the most skilled handling. These are the situations when adaptability serves the suppliers and tour managers at their best.

In nearly every case they were able to make immediate changes, create acceptable alternatives and, best of all, maintain the customers' confidence in the travel system. By staying well informed about conditions and events, travel planners can often produce ingenious results for unexpected problems.

Travel managers cannot ignore security and safety measures.

Throughout any crisis situation, travel/tourism is primarily concerned with the safety and well-being of customers and their belongings. They are eager to fulfill their commitments to service: time, location and connections. They know that it is critical to handle all funds with accuracy and integrity. All of this will ensure them of repeat business and customer loyalty.

One major change that has occurred in the past decade is in people's attitudes and responses to problems. The effects on travel may be subtle, but they are certainly not to be ignored as people become more aggressively "money-minded," causing them to justify every penny spent. Travel promotions, frequent flyer benefits, and bonuses are sought by all travel consumers. Even on a small budget, the client is

Liabilities

determined to receive the very best of services and will pursue the problem to litigation. With consumer rights so actively supported, travel firms and suppliers are giving full attention to legal consequences in all possible situations. Law suits by disappointed customers are costly and destructive to a firm's image, so all personnel involved need to be concerned.

The industry protects itself... and you.

Discussing these issues can be rather discouraging until you realize all of the ways that the profession is protected from risks. These concerns have been around throughout the history of travel, and responsible leaders have developed sound methods to prevent unmanageable problems.

The Role of Government

From the very beginning of air travel in the 1930s, the federal government has dealt with the need for safety practices as well as a system of retailing the operations of airlines. They set up the Civil Aeronautics Board (CAB) for just those purposes, with rigid rules about eligibility and safety for flight systems and areas of operation. At that time, there was no leisure air travel and very few international flights, so the system was workable.

In the years after World War II, air travel expanded quickly. Many new airlines developed, and the government created the Federal Aviation Administration (FAA). This office was responsible for licensing pilots, registering aircraft and setting rules to ensure passenger safety.

But the airlines had many other concerns. Suddenly there were thousands of customers to deal with for sales, reservations, and information. So they organized the Air Traffic Conference (ATC) to develop a system of travel agencies that could serve as their sales centers. They set up rules about the ways agencies had to function, and about the reporting of their businesses. The ATC also set limits and restrictions that controlled travel routes, fares and operation methods.

Needless to say, all of these regulations became complicated and, after much deliberation, the government passed the Deregulation Act in 1978. The safety rules still held, but it allowed airlines to decide among themselves when and where to schedule flights. Of course, it also opened competition so the public could have a wider variety of choices in planning their travel.

Meanwhile, the same kind of development was occurring with railroads and motorcoach systems. The Interstate Commerce Commission (ICC) was established to provide control over the interstate and intrastate schedules and routing. They too have gradually given nearly complete flexibility for their operations. It is easy to realize how important this freedom is for tour managers.

As in all professions, personnel in the travel and tourism business recognized the strength that was possible by establishing their own associations. Not only would it provide them contacts in the field, but it would also give members a way to share their ideas and concerns. More importantly, they needed an organization that could maintain a standard of quality services that would be symbolic of their profession.

The first of these associations to be formed was the American Society of Travel Agents (ASTA). Today, it is a huge national and international organization. Companies and individuals from all segments of the industry have qualified for membership and they display their affiliation with pride. Professionals in travel and tourism have a respect and confidence in ASTA representatives and in their dealings with them. Their logo is a symbol of their

Professional Organizations

commitment to their profession, and to the quality of service they offer.

It is heartening that ASTA maintains its world headquarters in Washington, D.C., and supports representatives in Congress for legislation that will benefit the industry. They will, no doubt, be strong participants in the upcoming White House Conference on Tourism which is scheduled for the fall of 1995.

ASTA has been particularly active in its Education and Training Department which offers instruction and training conferences. They also distribute numerous informative publications that are helpful to people in this field. They even maintain a scholarship foundation that promotes professional growth and excellence by providing funds (both undergraduate and graduate levels) to those who are pursuing travel and tourism careers.

There is another organization of this type that exists exclusively for retail travel agents and agencies. You may see them listed as the Association of Retail Travel Agents (ARTA). This organization functions in a similar fashion to help the agent handle problems through workshops and seminars.

Organizations For Tour Managers

As a prospective tour manager, you may be especially interested in trade associations that serve the special needs of tourism personnel. The largest of these is the National Tour Association (NTA). This organization operates within the United States and Canada to encourage quality tour planning and to protect its members. They also provide their members with informative publications and hold industry-wide workshops and seminars to advise them about changes and policies to protect their programs.

You will also meet tour operators who display their logo of United States Tour Operators Association (USTOA). This is a trade association with strict rules for membership including demonstrated sound business practices and financial stability. It is easy to understand why these matters are so important when you remember that a few irresponsible deals could affect many others in the industry.

Another organization that is particularly supportive of group tour operators is the American Bus Association. Although they represent the suppliers of motorcoach transportation, they recognize the operators as key figures in their business. They are also head-quartered in Washington D.C. and provide a strong lobby in behalf of tourism legislation. Watch for announcements of their workshops and seminars for tour leaders. The ABA also provides useful publications and a journal with up-to-date information.

Obviously, each responsible travel agency and tour operator will protect themselves with liability insurance, but they will also know that their affiliated agencies will stand by them in cases of serious concerns.

Summary

To review, we can conclude that the travel industry is healthy and has the ability to thrive in the 1990s. Careers in travel and tourism will always be changing in the way they function, but that is to be expected in a field that serves so many aspects of our ever-changing lives. The public will continue to travel for business, professional and leisure purposes. The greatest increases will undoubtedly be in the area of personal/leisure trips. These are encouraging trends for people in the tourism field.

Travel and tourism have survived the downturn in recent years because of these factors:

- They serve as agents or sales representatives for many other service businesses (suppliers).

- They are not restricted to specific suppliers, but have an ever growing variety from which they can choose.
- Travel tends to be seasonal in its operations, providing opportunities for adaptations for special needs.
- Creative marketing methods work well with the popular appeal that travel holds for consumers.
- Travel and tourism firms continue to be operated by personnel with required training and efficiency standards.
- They have the benefits of continued support through safety regulations and trade associations.

Careers in travel/tourism offer challenging opportunities plus enormous responsibilities. Travel personnel has been an important part of the survival experience in the 1990's. Successful firms rely upon their knowledge, business skills, and commitment to service.

Questions For Further Study

1. Make a list of the major travel agencies in your local community. Which agencies publicize their membership in ASTA? In ARTA?

2. List the major suppliers (hotels/motels, restaurants, car rental companies, attractions) that depend on travelers for their business volume.

3. Name any travel-related firms whose businesses have failed in the past 2 or 3 years.

4. What are the main features of your local area that draw tourists to your city?

Note: A visit to your local convention and visitors bureau might be a good source of this information.

UNDERSTANDING THE TOUR BUSINESS

CHAPTER TWO

Group tours developed early as a natural and inevitable offspring of the travel industry. They have grown to represent a profitable part of the travel business and account for more than 20 billion dollars spent in the United States. World-wide, the figures increase as international tourism thrives. The National Tour Association reports more than 600 companies as members.

Throughout the development of the travel industry, transportation has continued to be the important focus of their services. But gradually, all sorts of other traveler needs have become a part of the travel reservations and sales.

Of course, many clients still use the agency for a simple purchase of tickets. But many others have found how easy it is to arrange for a rental car or hotel room. They are glad to have their transfers ready and waiting and to be assured that the side-trip excursion is operating on that day. They can even reserve tickets to sporting events or various types of entertainment. Each traveler could arrange all of these on his own, and a few of them do, but it requires considerable time, effort, phone calls and uncertainty to get all of the plans put together.

It didn't take long for the firms producing all of these services to recognize some great marketing opportunities. Why not sell these services in combinations that would be

The Package Tour

even more appealing to clients? It would increase the volume of sales for all of the services. In the business world, volume in growing profits is the magic word.

And so the package tour was created. Combining the various travel services into packages that could be sold together was the beginning of the package tour. In fact, these combinations could then be offered at a special reduced price. This obviously made the package more attractive than ever.

The variety of combined features for the packages was endless. They could be offered according to the needs of the majority of the travelers. Packages could be planned around the services available at any specific destination, or even adapted to special events or seasons of the year. Since airlines, railroads and bus carrier systems provide most of the transportation, these were the first firms to promote special tour packages. They combined:

Packages can be planned around services available at any specific destination or even adapted to special events or seasons of the year

- Cross-country flight with a car rental creating a fly–drive package.
- Flight or railway trip with a steamship cruise for an air–sea package.
- Motorcoach trip to special events or sight seeing to become a getaway package.

There were other combinations that included accommodations at a hotel or motel, and sometimes appealing little "perks" like the use of the nearby golf course or tennis. These packages have continued to be popular because they allow the traveler the opportunity to depart and return just about any day they choose. Plus, they offer discounted travel at rates that have already been set.

These are called *independent tours* and they are designed for people who want to travel on their own, yet take advantage of the pre-arranged discounted prices. Travel agencies are able to sell these independent tour packages as easily as they would a simple airline ticket. The airline (or firm that pre-arranges the tour) is responsible for making sure that all of the services are available and they commission the agency for the sale. Actually, there is not much follow-through necessary on the services, except to confirm that the traveler will be reserved and scheduled at the reduced rates.

A tour, then, is a pre-arranged trip which uses the services of two or more supplier firms and is listed at a single price. The firm that packages these tour arrangements is called the *tour operator*. If it sells the packages only through travel agencies, it is a *tour wholesaler*. But sometimes such firms sell outright to the public, and then they are listed as tour operators.

Types of Tours

There are tour companies that specialize in tours using a specific mode of transportation. They may operate their entire trips by motorcoach or railway. Of course, motorcoaches are most commonly used for domestic tours, because they can reach a wide variety of locations. If a tour involves several types of transportation, it is called an **intermodal tour.**

Some operators arrange tours from the United States to other countries. They are referred to as **outbound operators**. They often set up their tour plans with the help of a **ground operator** in the location where the tour group is going. The outbound operator still carries the full responsibility for the success of the entire tour, but the ground operator is a valuable assistant in locating suppliers in a foreign setting and in helping to arrange details. Obviously the outbound operator needs to be fluent in languages and knowledgeable about foreign customs and currencies in order to negotiate all of the arrangements.

More and more tourists from other countries are visiting the United States. The situation in these cases suddenly becomes reversed. If they are traveling with a group, they need a ground operator for their trips around the country. If you choose to work with one of these inbound tourist groups, you are considered an **inbound operator.** Again, the role requires a different approach and the special ability to communicate about parts of our culture that we take for granted.

Inclusive Tours

As more and more features are added to a tour plan, it becomes classified as an **inclusive tour.** Some of these arrangements are more detailed, so they may require travelers to be assisted in getting around to parts of their tour sequence. In some locations, the tour operator schedules a local hospitality service or host to be available to help the tourists arrange their sight- seeing or to make special connections. This is especially important in unfamiliar areas or in foreign countries. In such cases, a language or currency difference could easily become a problem and a host would ease any special concerns.

Of course, the services of that local host will need to be paid, as will any of the other added features. So, as the inclusive tour becomes more desirable to the traveler, it will necessarily carry a higher price.

Tour operators have created ingenious ways to help independent travelers avoid difficulties. They offer a wide variety of maps, pamphlets and brochures as guides for sight-seeing. Sometimes, they may arrange a general city tour soon after arrival so the tourist can become oriented to the new location. Independent travelers are always provided with telephone numbers and names of contact persons who can help them in case of an emergency. It's easy to understand how the tourist values these considerations.

The Group Tour

As these pre-arranged trips begin to include more and more features, it becomes reasonable that they cannot be scheduled for just any date or time. Consider these examples:

- The main attraction may be a scheduled event, such as the Olympics competitions or the Passion Play in Oberammergau—rare opportunities.
- There may be many additional features that will drive up the costs. These cannot be absorbed into the price, unless a large number of people are going.
- Planning, reserving and scheduling become expensive factors, so the tour price cannot be justified if only a few people participate.

Therefore, the system ensures a quality inclusive tour at a reasonable price will involve groups. There are inevitable concerns that surface when groups of people travel together. However, most of these can be limited or prevented by using a **tour director** or **escort**. With large groups both are sometimes used. These individuals serve as leaders, guides and managers for the entire tour to make certain every part of the trip proceeds as planned.

The escorted group tour usually doesn't offer the freedom and flexibility of independent travel. Obviously, the dates and times for departures are set and most of the activities are shared by all group members. They usually stay at the same hotel/motel and attend the scheduled events together. Wise tour managers do plan numerous "on your own" periods of time or optional activities to help balance the concentrated "togetherness" effects.

The advantages of group tours outweigh the disadvantages on nearly every count:

- Careful planning has brought all of the components of

The escorted group tour usually doesn't offer the freedom and flexibility of independent travel.

The Values Of Group Travel

the tour into a workable sequence for a safe, rewarding experience.

- Each segment of transportation is scheduled.
- Transfers are arranged whenever needed.
- Comfortable lodging and quality meals are assured.
- Sightseeing trips are planned.
- Admission to entertainment and special events is certain.
- Special charges (tips, taxes and baggage handling) are paid.

The advantages of group tours outweigh the disadvantages on nearly every count.

Tour members are relieved of the responsibility for making the many decisions that often frustrate the individual traveler. Admittedly, choices have been made about what to see and where to go, but tour members can feel confident that quality experiences are included. The tour group will arrive at and depart from the entrance, with no parking hassles or fees. Their arrival is expected and they will be given plenty of time for leisurely and carefree enjoyment.

Best of all, the major costs of the trip are all pre-paid and the tour plan lets them know of any personal expenses that each member would need to pay. People are prone to underestimate the costs of travel and often neglect to consider the many miscellaneous charges they will face. Totaling all of these advantages with congenial companionship and dependable leaders, proves group touring is indeed an ideal and economical choice. It is no wonder that its popularity has grown so rapidly in recent years.

Group Discounts

The main reason that group touring is a profitable system is because suppliers of the various tour components cooperate so well. They consistently offer discounted prices to groups of a significant size. Each firm that offers a service for sale has his eye on the profit margin too. They have costs involved in providing that service, whether it be hotel accommodations, entertainment or transportation. One of their major costs is the marketing of their service. Advertising, selling, and scheduling the service costs the firm for each tour. These are necessary in order to be sure that their volume of sales stays at its best.

Through a group sale, forty, fifty or even hundreds of sales are made in one transaction and the price of the service can be discounted while their profit level still remains the same or, hopefully, increases.

Advantages For The Travel Agency

The travel agency gains by booking clients on a group tour. Again, a single tour reservation for a customer completes the sale. If such an involved trip had to be planned segment by segment through a travel agent it would require endless hours of effort. Even then, there would be no group discounts and limited commissions.

Occasionally, individuals or groups come to an agency with a request for a special custom-made tour. It usually involves a time frame or sequence of destinations that simply does not fit into any of the commercial tour plans available. In the travel business, if these tours are geared toward other countries they are referred to as Foreign Inclusive Tours (FIT). If the tours are within the United States, they are referred to as Domestic Inclusive Tours (DIT). While most travel agencies cannot afford the time and effort planning such a specialized tour, they may have a tour consultant on staff who can set up the necessary arrangements.

It might be possible that some existing independent tour schedule could be adapted and patched together for that client. But usually, the custom tour program needs a specialist who can work closely with the group and shape it into a reality.

Such individuals are valuable assets in the travel industry as there are many situations that call for their talent and experience.

Choosing Quality Tours

One of the best ways to evaluate the quality of a tour is by following up with customers who have traveled with that company.

With more than 350 major tour companies producing tours, you may wonder how any travel agent can become well enough informed about the available trips. All of the operators and wholesalers have their own sets of tours, and even those change from season to season. New itineraries are developed and prices changed. Besides, how could anyone know whether a certain company is reliable and offering quality tours?

Of course, the answer is they don't. So they need to use a number of resources to gradually get to know the tour companies and the reputations they have built. Travel agents try to find out how long a firm has been operating a successful business since that is a strong evidence of reliable performance. They learn to avoid making reservations with companies that frequently cancel tours or change prices and itineraries. Such practices are frustrating to clients and to the agents who book them, and it certainly does not encourage repeat business.

One of the best ways to evaluate the quality of a tour is by following up with customers who have traveled with that company. When satisfied clients give consistently enthusiastic reports, we can usually feel confident that the tour firm is offering quality trips. Companies realize that this is true and often include such positive endorsements in their advertising materials. Tour operators also frequently send representatives from their staffs to trade shows and travel conventions. They know that travel retailers are valuable contacts and make every effort to build strong business relations with them.

The most common means of learning about available tours is by studying the current brochures. Usually colorful, artistic and hopefully informative, these are advertising booklets or leaflets that tour companies distribute describing their tours. An up-to-date file of these provides excellent references. Incidentally, those brochures are also a good resource for tour planners who are seeking ideas for appealing destinations and activities.

Tour brochures also include valuable information that can

indicate whether the company has a good record and if it is financially stable. Here are some fairly good clues:

(a) Does the brochure state that the tour operator is a member of one of the national associations? Many of these organizations limit members to companies who offer escorted tours throughout North America. To belong, members must operate within an established code of ethics and post a liability bond to prevent losses in financial dealings.

(b) If the company offers worldwide tours, does it list a membership in USTOA (United States Tour Operators Association)? This membership requires a minimum of three years of successful operation under the same management. They must also have an established business volume and carry one million dollars worth of liability insurance.

(c) Finally, does the tour operator hold a membership in ASTA (American Society of Travel Agents)? If so, they have demonstrated their ability as a company and have posted a bond to protect their clients who have reserved and paid for booking on tours.

There are also some excellent catalogues of both domestic and word-wide tours. These are very helpful in searching out possibilities for existing tours. Request from:

Official Airlines Guides (OAG)
2000 Clearwater Drive Dept. J921
Oakbrook, Illinois 60521-9953
They have available:
- Worldwide Tour Guide
- North American Tour Guide
- Travel Planner (Hotel and Motel Guide)
- North American Edition
- European Edition
- Pacific/Asia Edition

An up-to-date file of brochures provides excellent reference material.

A recent development in the tour business offers a promising means of locating automated information about tours. One California-based firm has set up a computerized electronic system that displays current tours and rates from various companies. It also provides automatic reservations and bookings for the tours that are listed. It still isn't as complete and trouble-free as the travel agent's central processing unit used for airline reservations, but in the coming months and years *Tourinc* (its trade name) will undoubtedly be an enormous help to travel counselors and their tour-oriented clients.

Good marketing ideas are quickly adopted by other branches of the industry. Cruise operators are now developing a similar booking system called *Cruisinc*. It will assist travel agents in their search for cruises by listing all of the options for the various cruise lines. They can check points of departure, ports of call, prices and departure dates. They may even request cabin types, dining room seating, and special meals as they book the cruise. Such automated systems are a boost to the customer and agency, as well as the growing number of cruise lines.

Trends play an important role in the travel industry.

As you would expect, the trends of the 1990s are affecting tour businesses, too. During the past few years, economic conditions in Europe have become extremely volatile. These countries are closely tied in economic matters and as a crises develops in one, immediate financial pressures arise in the others. According to the USTTA figures, inbound tourism declined by 3.7% last year, reflecting decreases especially from England and Germany. But recessions in other countries such as Canada, Mexico, and Japan are also taking their toll so it may be a while before inbound tourism is on the rise. Overseas (outbound) travel by Americans, however, was up by 5% in 1993 and predicated for a 3% increase in 1994.

There are also trends toward different kinds of tour preferences that tour operators may need to consider. Budget conscious customers are attracted to group tours with a specified price for the complete trip. In fact, a recent study reported in Travel Weekly indicated that all-inclusive tours had increased the most of all types. It appears that people want to be sure they may have as many choices as possible.*

For those travelers with middle and upper incomes, the choices for tours are increasingly the independent package tours. Flexibility appeals to them, with the choice to use their time as they wish. Among escorted tours, many travelers are in fact looking at plans that provide more optional periods of free time so they can pursue their own interests. On the other hand, tour members are seeking opportunities for active participation in events, instead of simply sight-seeing and picture taking.

One of the most significant preferences among tour clients is for experienced and responsible tour operators. Perhaps they have been dismayed once too often by the trimmed-down, no frills bargains they had sought. Inexperienced group leaders who plan low cost tours for their local organizations are frequently unaware of critical concerns about safety and financial responsibility. Emergencies and unexpected problems are simply beyond their abilities and resources. Therefore, smart consumers are recognizing the importance of tour operators that represent reliable firms.

One of the most significant preferences among tour c lients is for experienced and responsible tour operators.

Changes in types of bookings of tour & vacation packages

FACTOR	Increased	Decreased	Remained The Same
Fully Escorted	21%	26%	53%
Hosted (with city stays)	26%	20%	54%
All inclusive (with air)	60%	11%	29%
Fly Drive	43%	15%	42%
FIT'S (Foreign Independent Tours)	44%	21%	35%
Independent Packages	51%	7%	42%

* Del Rosso, Laura, One Stop Shopping - Travel Weekly, Dec. 31, 1992

Summary

The development of the package tour was the beginning of a strong and enduring part of the travel industry. Through the years, it has taken on many different forms, but it has brought unlimited opportunities for creative plans and financial profit. By staying aware of consumer needs and preferences, tour managers will continue to offer the tours that the traveling public seeks.

Questions For Further Study

A good way to learn about various types of tours is by studying their brochures. Obtain a few from your nearby travel agency and see how much information they provide. On page 28, you will find a tour description taken from a current brochure of Brendan Tours. This is an example of an independent (hosted) tour. Study it carefully to find the answers to these questions.

1. Each tour firm assigns numbers and letters to each tour for reference purposes. What is the letter code for this tour? What is the number of the tour scheduled for August 4?

2. Throughout the tour description, meals that are included in the tour price are designated as follows: CB - Continental Breakfast; BB - Buffet Breakfast' FB - Full Breakfast; L - Lunch; D - Dinner. How many meals are included in this tour price?

3. What services will the tour host provide during the whole week?

4. Note that all prices are listed in U.S. dollars. Note also that prices vary from very early spring to very late autumn. List the months that represent the popular (high) season in Paris. What percent higher will costs tend to be in the high season?

5. Notice that prices are listed for round trips from U.S. but in the 4th column, prices are listed for "land only" costs (for those who will join and leave the tour in Paris). From these two columns, figure the airfare costs in low season. How much is it in high season?

6. What other costs will tour members be required to pay for themselves on this tour? Can you estimate approximately what the entire trip will cost the average tour member?

STAY PUT
A WEEK IN PARIS

*8 days including air
or 7 days in Paris*

Sacre-Coeur, Paris

BRENDAN'S TRAVEL VALUE INCLUDES

- Scheduled transatlantic flights and airport transfers in Paris if Brendan Tours issues the tickets; see page 12
- Host service throughout your stay; on arrival you receive a welcome wallet including a city map and other valuable information
- Twin-bedded rooms with private bath at the Novotel Paris Les Halles, hotel taxes, service charges and tips for baggage handling
- Welcome drink; buffet breakfast (BB) daily
- Guided half-day sightseeing including the Eiffel Tower and Notre Dame
- Specially arranged discounts at the famous Galeries Lafayette department stores, Parfumerie Eden, and other leading shops
- Brendan Tours travel bag and portfolio of travel documents

Novotel Paris Les Halles

Place Marguerite de Navarre
F-75001 Paris

A modern first-class hotel with 285 rooms.

Location: On the site of the historic market in the very heart of the city, next to a vast shopping complex and the famous Pompidou Center, and within walking distance of the Louvre.

Its sound-proofed and air-conditioned rooms feature private bath, shower and toilet, direct-dial telephone, color TV, radio alarm clock, and mini-bar.

Elegant public areas include the Garden Bar and La Rotisserie, a fine restaurant in the French tradition.

ITINERARY

Day 1, Fri. BOARD YOUR OVERNIGHT TRANSATLANTIC FLIGHT.

Day 2, Sat. ARRIVAL IN PARIS, FRANCE. The day is free to rest or start exploring the splendid French capital. Later today join your host for a welcome drink.

Day 3, Sun. PARIS. Your half-day tour with a local expert includes sights on both banks of the Seine: Arc de Triomphe, Opéra, Madeleine, Louvre, Champs-Elysées . . . For a panoramic view, take the elevator to the first floor of the **Eiffel Tower.** Of course, you also visit Paris' greatest treasure, the Gothic cathedral of **Notre Dame** with its gleaming stained-glass windows. Afternoon at leisure. (BB)

Days 4 - 7, Mon. - Thu. AT LEISURE IN PARIS. Four more days to discover what this extraordinary metropolis has to offer. Explore the world capital of chic and style at your own pace. Visit the fashion houses and boutiques, take your pick from 90 fine museums, including the Louvre, stroll through magnificent parks, promenade along the Champs-Elysées . . . You'll never run out of things to do and see. If you want to go further afield, join an optional excursion to the lavish Baroque palace of Versailles or to the great impressionist Claude Monet's home in the

Seine Valley. After dark, check out some of the great gourmet restaurants and irresistible revue shows. Ask your local host for suggestions and reservations. (BB daily)

Day 8, Fri. YOUR HOMEBOUND FLIGHT ARRIVES THE SAME DAY. (BB)

Tour DP —
DEPARTURES & PRICES

Tour Number	Leave USA Friday	Return to USA Friday	7 Days Land Cost US$	8 Days USA/USA US$
0325	Mar 24	Mar 31	$678	$1158
0401	Mar 31	Apr 07	$688	$1179
0408	Apr 07	Apr 14	$698	$1355
0415	Apr 14	Apr 21	$708	$1365
0422	Apr 21	Apr 28	$718	$1375
0429	Apr 28	May 05	$718	$1375
0506	May 05	May 12	$718	$1375
0513	May 12	May 19	$718	$1375
0520	May 19	May 26	$718	$1375
0527	May 26	Jun 02	$718	$1381
0603	Jun 02	Jun 09	$718	$1512
0610	Jun 09	Jun 16	$718	$1512
0617	Jun 16	Jun 23	$718	$1512
0624	Jun 23	Jun 30	$718	$1512
0701	Jun 30	Jul 07	$718	$1512
0708	Jul 07	Jul 14	$718	$1512
0715	Jul 14	Jul 21	$718	$1512
0722	Jul 21	Jul 28	$718	$1512
0729	Jul 28	Aug 04	$718	$1512
0805	Aug 04	Aug 11	$718	$1512
0812	Aug 11	Aug 18	$718	$1512
0819	Aug 18	Aug 25	$718	$1512
0826	Aug 25	Sep 01	$718	$1512
0902	Sep 01	Sep 08	$718	$1512
0909	Sep 08	Sep 15	$718	$1512
0916	Sep 15	Sep 22	$718	$1506
0923	Sep 22	Sep 29	$718	$1375
0930	Sep 29	Oct 06	$718	$1375
1007	Oct 06	Oct 13	$718	$1375
1014	Oct 13	Oct 20	$708	$1365
1021	Oct 20	Oct 27	$698	$1355
1028	Oct 27	Nov 03	$688	$1334
1104	Nov 03	Nov 10	$678	$1158

Single room supplement: $285
Triple room reduction per person: $66

Extra nights per person: in single room $155; in twin room $100; in triple room $84.

For any air fare supplement from your U.S. departure city, see page 168 (List 4).

THE TOUR OPERATOR

Throughout history, groups of people have traveled together and found that it was an effective system. Hundreds trudged the miles to worship at a sacred shrine. The masses converged to witness a coronation or other historical event. Pioneers formed groups to travel by wagon train, bound for the golden West. Whatever their purposes, members were together because they had discovered that group travel provided them companionship, economy and safety. Although our modern package tours offer much more, these are still the main reasons for their success.

We occasionally hear reports of people who have been disappointed in their tour experience, but most reactions are positive. Tour operators are aware that a satisfied customer is the best ambassador for future business, so they give first priority to customer needs and expectations.

Tour organizers tend to be energetic, creative individuals. Whether they are staff members for a large tour company or an independent tour planner, their challenge is the same. Each season, they need to originate plans that will capture the imagination of participants. They hope to choose appealing destinations with fascinating activities and complete each trip with an optimum profit level.

Through the years, successful tour operators have developed systems for sound organization and marketing procedures. These are based on principles of business management, well-seasoned with common sense and human concern. The system is built around an orderly sequence of tasks that will coordinate all of the services into a smooth operation.

Conceptualization

You may be surprised to learn how many months of advanced planning are required for a tour to become a reality. Most companies are shaping their schedules at least a season in advance — sometimes even a year or so. Staff members are accustomed to this necessity and depend on the top-level decisions that become the framework for each season.

Managing officers of the firm schedule meetings with representatives from each of the staff units in marketing, advertising and sales. They also need input from the tour director and escorts, for every pertinent suggestion that may be helpful.

1st Stage

This "think tank" group has been assembled to make decisions about the upcoming season's program of tour offerings. It is extremely important because these decisions will mean the difference between profits and losses, successes or failures.

So, what are the topics in this lively discussion? First, the manager outlines the scope and limitations of the tours to be considered according to the business plan of the company. This is the reality statement about the financial and personnel resources that will be available to produce the tours. There may also need to be a reminder about the established regions, countries, and customer groups that will be served. This information helps to keep the meeting on considered tour possibilities that are reasonable and practical.

Next the meeting group will review the previous season's tour reports. Which were successful? Disappointing? Worth repeating this year? Possible with some adaptations? These are all recorded for consideration.

Soon suggestions are beginning to emerge for new tour destinations: a city, a country, or general area of interest. It may be an attraction such as a new Disney theme park to be opened or a bicentennial festival in a certain state or country. Or perhaps the tour would feature an area that offers many points of interest such as the Old South with its abundant azalea gardens, historic homes and the ethnic charm of New Orleans. Occasionally, an idea comes from a client suggestion or from a customer group that is exploring preferred places to go.

Each suggestion triggers questions from members of the group. They each have a "stake" in every plan as it indicates what they will need to do to make it happen. Will there be appropriate lodging, meals or ground transportation and at what prices? Is there safe, convenient group transportation to and from that destination on those dates and at what prices? Considering the consumer public, can enough interest be generated to sell the tour for the anticipated profits?

Most companies are shaping their schedules at least a season in advance.

2nd Stage

By the next meeting, the group has put in a lot of hours to bring more tangible information on which they can base their decisions. Some factors are definite deterrents — others are simply problems which they can work through. Some destinations can definitely be eliminated and others look promising. It may take further sessions, but it looks as if final decisions can soon be made.

3rd Stage

The trip is still just a proposal until the planning personnel check out the realities. They are selling the services of suppliers, some of which they have never heard. What is the quality of the services that can be provided? What levels of group discounted prices will the various suppliers be able to

Working Out Details

offer? Will there be space available on the dates being considered? It will probably be necessary for some members of the planning group to go to the destination to get first-hand information.

4th Stage

Finally, the planners have eliminated all of the "unknowns" and "uncertainties." Contacts have been made with supplier representatives and definite prices have been agreed upon. As all parts of the plan for each tour is approved, that package is created. Definite dates have been determined for each tour as well.

6th Stage

All this time, the marketing staff has been developing their strategies for presenting and promoting each of the tours for the season. Often they combine the offerings into a brochure to be distributed to prospective buyers. Advertising personnel are exploring all possible techniques for promoting the available tours through the media. They are constantly searching for innovations that will appeal to buyers, both new customers and repeat travelers.

Financial Operations

7th Stage

Every tour company has to establish a procedure to follow as customers reserve and purchase their tours. Accounting departments must establish and maintain accurate files on each member of each tour.

They have to be provided with confirmation, receipts, instructions and detailed information about the actual day-to-day procedures of the trip.

8th Stage

Relationships with the suppliers are especially important throughout the whole sales period. Each firm that is supplying a service has to be apprised of the number of tour members to expect, along with any special instructions. Suppliers must also be paid (at least a deposit and sometimes in full) to assure them that the group will be using the service as it was contracted.

Occasionally, it becomes certain that there will not be enough tour reservations sold to justify operating the tour. In that case, cancellations with each supplier are necessary, and must be done within the time limits of the contracts that were negotiated.

9th Stage

It often appears that a tour leader or escort has little or no responsibility before the tour group departs on the trip. Nothing could be further from the truth. Throughout this whole planning and sales period, there are preparations to be made. If it is an unfamiliar destination the task is even more challenging. Soon, he/she will have the responsibility for directing large numbers of tourists from location to location. There will be questions to answer and details for reminders. Yes, there will always be some unexpected circumstances to handle too, so the more prepared they are, the better.

It is ideal for the tour leader or escort to visit the destination in advance. They need to collect all of the information available about it. Guides from the Convention and Visitors' Bureau (pamphlets on significant sites, conversations with their promoters. etc.) will be valuable resources to the tour leader or escort. For that interval of time when the tour is in progress, he/she will be trying to function as knowledgeable hosts and competent leaders of the group.

This trip, with this group, will only occur this time, so it is the escort's single chance to give them his/her very best effort.

Conducting The Tour

Summary & Evaluation

10th Stage

An important part of every tour is the summary information. After this enormous concerted effort, every staff member needs to share in the satisfactions of a successful tour. Of course they also deserve the information about improvements that need to be made so they can learn and grow in confidence.

The summary information includes:

- financial figures, contracted costs profits, etc.
- quality of services from the selected suppliers
- positive and negative responses from tour members
- recommendations for changes that would be appropriate for future trips to that destination

Records of this type are filed for future reference and for a possible repeat tour schedule.

As you may suspect, highly successful tours may be offered several times in one season, or at least yearly. Much of the costly tour preparations have been done, so repeated tours are more profitable if there is continued public demand.

This involved sequence of steps in tour operation may seem to be complex and very detailed. But you can be sure that each step is absolutely necessary. Can you imagine the consequences, when you arrive at a Holiday Inn with 40 weary passengers only to discover that the reservations have not been held because the deposit was not paid? Certainly, "no room at the inn" is not going to generate a very congenial attitude and probably some very frustrating problems. Even on simple one- or two- day excursions, these procedures are equally important. They just won't be as complex or time consuming.

From the sequence of steps that are listed you can understand the roles of each person involved in the development of a tour. With each trip, the employees gain valuable experience and knowledge about the procedures; they learn names of contact persons in various firms; they become aware of policies and problems and they are more prepared to deal with the next situations that arise.

In very much the same way, travel agents often find their way into tour management. Their background and training is an excellent foundation for the activities in tour planning and management.

People who plan to work as independent tour operators or consultants may not find the path so smooth. Without much background in the travel industry, they will need to focus on learning as much as possible about it. At the same time, they will be engaging in a new business venture. So it is wise for them to proceed cautiously and diligently.

Travel agents often find their way into tour management.

All people who hope to succeed in the travel industry need to have certain qualities to help them function well. They need a well-rounded educational background and a genuine enjoyment of learning. They need to stay abreast of current events that will be useful in their planning and decisions every day. Topics are endless, from geography or international issues to trends in the stock market.

Since there are so many business transactions involved in the travel industry, it is obvious that all workers must understand and function well in the business setting. They need skills in negotiating with suppliers and in dealings with clients and co-workers, as well. Some business contacts are brief, momentary calls for information, but most of them are continuing business relationships. All of them shape a professional style of operation.

Tour planning and management calls for some special attitudes and skills, such as:

- The ability to originate innovative plans with realistic possibilities for group tour experiences. Equally important is the flexibility to adapt plans and find workable alternatives when it is necessary.

**Tour managers
need skills for
effective business
negotiations.**

- The skill to organize long range plans. Weeks and months of advanced arrangements are often required, so tour managers must be patient and persistent. Seeing the entire project through, with careful attention to details is critical to the success of the tour.
- The knowledge and ability to lead and interact with groups effectively. This is considerably more than simply being congenial and sociable. Groups are combinations of many different personalities. Good leadership methods create cooperative, enthusiastic tour groups — the ultimate goal of the entire program.

Undoubtedly, these are abilities that grow with months and years of learning and experience. Each prospective tour leader will need to decide whether this line of work will be satisfying to him/her. These are factors well-worthy of consideration.

Questions for Further Study

1. Make a list of all of the factors that are necessary for a certain destination to be a promising tour.

2. What are the qualifications necessary for:
   – staff members who work in marketing tours?
   – tour leaders and escorts?

3. What kinds of mistakes or errors might become problems for the independent tour operator?

CHOICES & DECISIONS

Decisions about your career are some of the most important choices of your lifetime. They determine how much training you will need and how many years of schooling you will include. They control your chances for employment and for the advancements that will be possible in the years ahead. Most of all, they shape the situations in which you will work throughout your employment years.

Unfortunately, our society gives these momentous decisions to the persons who are least prepared for them. Young people with little understanding of any career field are pressed to make their choices. However, most of them must depend on suggestions by family, friends or a school counselor. An assortment of college catalogues or a persuasive recruiter will round out their resources.

Is it any wonder that more than half of these young people will drift into careers that will become unsatisfying to them? Experts maintain that a prime reason for job stress is the lack of personal satisfaction that the employee receives from the work that he is doing. Is it a further surprise that the quality of job performance for these people is less than expected?

Many career years are wasted by workers who deplore "If I had only known" and society loses through these misdirected talents. Now let's consider some preventions:

- Learn as much as you can about the whole field of work that you are considering.
- Discover the major goals that created the field and keep it going.
- Find the ways those purposes fit with your own values and interests.

Unless you really believe in the importance of a job, it is hard to keep your dedication to it through the years. Every career field has a variety of work that needs to be done. As you learn about these, you should find out what each job type involves. That means the kinds of routine tasks and special responsibilities. Yes, even the irritating, annoying and frustrating aspects that are there. If you are attracted to only one type of job in a field, the chances are not as likely that you will find that special opening. Probably too, you would not advance in the company as easily.

Incidentally, current trends in employment show that certain types of jobs can become obsolete in a decade or less. Keeping yourself versatile in your job field may rule out the costly need to retrain and start over in a new vocation.

The Tour Management Field

Now, let's apply all of this thinking to a career in tour management.

The preceding chapters have given you an overview of the travel/tourism industry. By this time you can understand how it has become such a complex field. You also recognize the social and economic trends that affect this type of work. As we explore the actual development of a tour, it is easier to see the variety of talents that are necessary.

Where Do You Fit Into This Picture?

First, we need to identify just what your motivations are, as you consider a career in tourism. Prospective students usually respond with these remarks:

> *"I love to travel and value the
> benefits of tourism programs"*

> *"People in that business get to travel everywhere
> free — and members of their families too"*

> *"You get to see fascinating places all
> over the world and meet interesting people"*

> *"I enjoy working with people"*

These remarks are common perceptions about work in tourism, but not a very accurate basis for a career choice. This is a field that is focused on business, and to be successful, tour managers must devote a large part of their time to business concerns and office procedures. The days that you actually lead groups of people on trips are a relatively small percentage of your time. Even then, the tours may be repeated to the same destination and become somewhat routine.

The notion that travel/tourism firms provide all employees with free or discounted travel is far from accurate. Those privileges are available in most agencies to certain eligible staff members. That means the full-time employee who has completed a specified number of months or years of service will be given that status. Of course, any staff member who must travel to set up their tours or other business activities would be reimbursed. But no travel employee can assume that he/she will be assured free or discounted travel.

There are tour companies that offer special programs for travel agents and tour specialists, so they can visit a new destination and become acquainted with a new tour. These are called familiarization trips, and are usually offered at a significant discount to travel personnel.

The days that you actually lead groups of people on trips are a relatively small percentage of your time

None of these travel industry "perks" is automatically extended to include family and friends of the employees. Unfortunately, your relatives usually do not understand these limitations, so they may eagerly seek those benefits. It will be your responsibility to explain the situation.

In general, employment opportunities in the tour business are fairly well defined by the stages we discussed in tour development. If your interests and aptitudes are stronger in a particular part of the business you would probably seek employment in that department. But, if you hope to gain experience and skills so that some day you'll be able to operate your own tour business, then you will need to be competent in all aspects of the tour business. Even though you may hire employees to carry out some parts of the tour program you will need experience and skills in those areas too.

Administration and Management Staff

Administrative staff may be one or several persons who have authority about discussions to be made and the general business plan. Their responsibilities extend far beyond the actual tour plan to facility management, employee supervision and financial deliberations.

Qualifications for Management

The individual in this position must have completed course work in Practical Economics, Marketing and Promotion, Budget and Finance, Sales Management and Customer Service. He/she may have been lucky enough to have access to a travel/tourism curriculum at the local or nearby college or university. Programs are also available at community/junior colleges and at vocational/proprietary schools.

These programs are taught by experienced travel/tourism professionals (usually 3-5 years of service required.) The content of the programs vary, but all of them are focused on professional competence in the travel industry. The American Society of Travel Agents has established a foundation, which encourages excellence in travel school programs. A list of approved schools in the United States and Canada can be obtained by writing to:

American Society of Travel Agents Foundation
P.O. Box 23992, Washington, D.C. 20026-3992

It would also be helpful to the prospective tour manager to be:

- computer literate
- knowledgeable about taxes and tariffs
- effective in communication

Experience is particularly important to these young professionals, so they need to search out every possible field experience. Some travel/tour companies set up liaison programs with the schools so students can fill in at a business during peak periods. Whether it is on a salary or volunteer basis, it becomes a valuable win-win situation. The company benefits from the help, and the student gains experience and contacts. Often, this opens doors for future employment. Being part of a management staff gives them the chance to see how plans are negotiated, before they have to face the full responsibility alone.

Marketing and Promotion Staff

For the person who thrives on the business aspects of tourism, a position in marketing would be ideal. Their background would have included similar courses, but the focus would be in financial management of the firm. Promotion, advertising and publications are the focus of their concern. Marketing experts are challenged to come up with creative and forceful strategies, so it is a unique kind of work.

Some travel/tour companies set up liaison programs with schools.

Clerical and Accounting Staff

As in all businesses, there is an enormous amount of record keeping, correspondence and routine financial maters to be handled in the tour business. Obviously, the staff in this division must be computer-competent and accurate in details.

The excellence of the clerical staff is primarily in the area of business procedures. However, their duties actually facilitate the work of the other departments. They must be astute learners of the polices and procedures in travel/tourism, as well as effective clerical aids.

Planning and Escorting Staff

Each of the departments of a tour company has a unique and critical part in making the tour program a success. But the planning and escort personnel has the job of making each tour a quality experience with all of the special features that will make it memorable.

These staff members need a general knowledge of the administrative and financial aspects of the business. They will need to be able to relate the financial plans to the actual components of the tour. In addition, they must work closely with marketing and accounting as the trips become realities. Tour planners are responsible for the day-by-day, hour-by-hour activities of each tour. This schedule, called the itinerary, is the framework of the entire trip. It involves time management, organization of ability, problem solving and decision making. For each tour, they must know details about each destination and be skilled in dealing with people of all ages. Quite a challenge!

A training program for tour managers needs to include study in:

- geography, (national and international)
- basic tour management techniques
- business relationships and ethics

> **Each of the departments of a tour company has a unique and critical part in making the tour program a success**

- psychology of working with groups
- sales techniques

You might be surprised to find tour managers as part of a sales staff. But that is exactly where most of them spend much of their life. These are people who contact group representatives to generate their interest in a travel project for their organization. Or, they may be visiting former group clients to encourage repeat tour business again this year. These are called outside sales contacts initiated by the sales staff themselves.

In contrast, there are other groups that contact the sales office with a request for a particular destination, date and activity. This is a custom tour and is classified as an inside sales contact. All of these responsibilities require effective salesmanship techniques.

In smaller tour companies the planning staff also serve as escorts — to actually accompany the group on the trip. Larger firms may find it more efficient to employ persons to serve only as escorts. They are sometimes also called guides or leaders. They are informed about the detailed plans of the itinerary in advance and the success of the tour is in their hands.

As you might guess, escorts frequently have considerable inactive time between tours so the company may employ them as part-timers, paid on the basis of days of service. Then, to make the income more financially stable, the escort may need to take on other part-time assignments for other tour companies. There are disadvantages to this arrangement. As a multiple part timer, the escort may never be eligible for company benefits, such as health insurance, retirement plans, and tenure eligibility. People who plan to become escorts need to negotiate carefully on matters of employment. Many of them solve the arrangement by being independent suppliers of escort services to tour firms. Then, through their own business, they can provide themselves with benefits as they are needed.

The Independent Tour Operator

There are individuals or couples who decide that they prefer to set up tour programs on their own by managing the number, size and types of tours themselves. They conclude that their work would be more rewarding personally and financially.

Some of these people have worked for tour companies and gained a wide variety of experiences in all aspects of the business. They are aware of the pitfalls and precautions as they can establish a strong viable business. They also know how and where to seek the help and advice they will need. Although they may start out as a small business, their future growth and profits are limited only by the time, energy, money and creativity they invest. At the same time, the full responsibility for success of the tour programs rests entirely with the owners. If they are willing to take risks and can afford the liability insurance necessary, they have a good chance for success.

Some independent operators affiliate with a travel agency to serve as their supplier for group tours. Here, they can share the resources of the agency, even though they will need to share their profits. Again, a carefully framed contract is necessary.

The "Dabbler"

That's what the tourist industry calls people who drift into tour management by circumstance. The individual who becomes "travel chairman" for his/her organization fits this pattern. He may have done considerable traveling on his own and relishes the opportunity to lead a group, especially when he can travel at no cost. After a few manageable group trips, this person feels confident that he can operate well on his own.

But lack of training and experience can easily become a serious threat, especially if funding is limited. Unexpected problems, accidents and costly law suits are simply not worth the gamble. A single incident can destroy his business hopes and dreams. The tour industry does not encourage "dabblers" for their own protection and for the image of the profession.

Which Route to Take?

If you are seriously considering a career in tour management, it is time to choose your route. First, you need to decide which aspect of the business fits you best. Each person is unique in his/her aptitudes and interests. People who follow a route that is satisfying and rewarding are invariably the most successful career-wise.

Whether you are planning your first career or changing fields after years in another kind of work, you need to allow yourself time to get the necessary background. You already have a head-start though, if you have:

- a good school record, completing secondary school
- some college courses, including basic business management, marketing, and advertising
- computer programming competency
- speech and communications courses
- knowledge of geography–U.S. and world
- psychology of human relations

Experience in Business or Sales

Check out the local colleges, universities and technical schools to determine which of them have courses that would supplement those you have. Even if they do not offer a travel/tourism curriculum, you can very likely shape your own course sequences that will prepare you. During your course work, you will definitely benefit by volunteering part-time with a tour operator in your local area. All experience is

All experience is valuable, but even better if it is in the phase of the tour business you hope to pursue.

valuable, but even better if it is in the phase of the tour business you hope to pursue.

For example, if you hope to be a tour planner, ask to sit in on some of their staff planning sessions. If you plan to become an escort, you might take a seasonal job as a tour guide for an established repeated tour. Firms employ these persons on tour buses for city and vicinity tours. Or they might be needed for attractions, such as theme parks, or state and national parks. Their tours are basic with pre-set routines and commentaries. The tour guides job is usually repetitive, but without many problems. This is an excellent means to gain experience.

Working with the staff of a tour company is a good way to develop tour management skills. You learn the terminology, the established procedures and expectations, and other staff members are usually most helpful in sharing your concerns.

During this preparation year, you will have a wonderful opportunity to know more about yourself as a future tour manager. You may have believed that you would enjoy setting up an itinerary on tour plan in detail. But when circumstances develop and call for a lot of changes, can you be flexible enough to handle them and "keep your cool"?

You may have believed that you were a "people- person" but come to realize that groups of people often involve some folks that can be demanding and critical. Even the most service-minded tour managers must learn how to deal with them.

And, in the last analysis, as a tour manager you will probably do considerable traveling, but it may not be to the destinations you had hoped and dreamed for. Instead, you'll be taking groups to places of their choice because that's what the tour business is all about.

What can you offer to the tourism industry? Take some time out to consider your own aptitude for this career. You will need:

Activity for Further Study

Knowledge

List the courses you have taken that will be useful to you in tour management positions?

Name of Course:	What I learned:	Will be helpful in:
(For example) Geography	Location of scenic sites Important major cities	Planning places tours & activities

Experience

List your experience (either work or personal) that you can rely on to help you in work with group tours?

Experience (describe)	Will help when I need to:
(For example) 1 year - clerk in drug store Managed sales, assisted inventory	Relate to customers Function in sales procedures

Personal Qualities

List your personal strengths that will be most helpful to you in your tourism work?

Personal quality	Advantage in tourism work:
(For example) • I am always prompt for schedules • I find it easy to talk with people of all ages	I can work within time schedules Relating to clients will be easy for me

Sometimes, even with adequate training and personal commitment there are certain conditions in your life that limit your ability to pursue a particular kind of work in tours. Which of these would you need to consider?

Situation:	Limitation in job choice:
(For example) A single parent with 2 children	I would need to avoid travel that involves overnights.

As you review your lists, you can now more easily define the type of tourism work that would be best suited to you. Consider them carefully and identify your niche(s) in the group tour business.

In a tour operator firm	As an independent tour manager
(For example) Administrator/ Manager Marketing/ salesperson Financial manager Clerical staff (bookkeeping/accounting) Tour manager/planner Escort or guide	All responsibilities are carried by the manager or by assistants employed as needed.

(Note) Remember that as you grow and learn in any of these job assignments, you gain the ability to advance into other positions within the company. Most employers encourage their staff members to attend in-service workshops and seminars so they can be ready for new and challenging opportunities.

DEVELOPING YOUR CLIENTELE

CHAPTER FIVE

Business managers rejoice when they realize that their customer files are expanding with loyal and enthusiastic followings. All businesses, whether dealing in products or services, depend heavily on their buying public. Quality products and profitable services are not worth creating unless they fill a demand by prospective buyers. Billions of dollars are spent each year by firms in their continued efforts to locate more customers. Advertising and media campaigns are constant reminders of their efforts.

A large part of travel marketing is accomplished with the needs of the individual traveler in mind:

- The service is created by the supplier.
- The travel agency makes the service available to the client.
- The client selects the service that fills his needs.
- The purchase is agreed and payment made.
- The service is provided to the buyer.

The service varies with each customer, the date and time to depart, the type of transportation, the destination, every aspect is arranged with the special needs and preferences of the traveler as a priority.

Group tours are marketed in a very different way, however. Here the trip is planned in advance to provide for a number of people, and the main elements of the tour are the

A group is
a number
of persons who
have certain
characteristics
and interests in
common.

same for every one of the clients. It might seem that group travel is planned without much concern about the participants' needs, but that is far from the truth since the competent tour manager focuses a great deal of attention to that very important matter.

This would be a good point for us to define our terms. When you refer to group travel, people often respond with a remark that all public travel serves groups these days, or more accurately "crowds." Their daily or weekly struggle through the jammed subway train or airport does not leave them with a positive attitude about groups. Obviously, these are masses of individuals who happen to be using the same service at the same time.

According to Webster, "a group is a number of persons who have certain characteristics and interests in common." Consider this example: A plane or train is heading for Denver loaded with people who all plan to arrive at the same terminal. They all have similar seating, identical meals, and even watch the same in-flight movie. But these folks are not a group because they have absolutely no bonds or shared interests. Even the casual passenger conversations are usually of no consequence, and as soon as their baggage is lifted from the carousel, each is on his own separate way, with his own purposes and plans. They have little concern about the other travelers.

When a tour operator initiates a new business, he/she needs to explore the entire sales area, to determine all possible groups of people that could become buyers. Some groups are well established organizations, that are well known in the community. They may be chapters of state or national organizations, such as Moose Lodge, A.A.R.P., Business and Professional Clubs, Rotary and Zonta. Many of them have community service projects, but they exist primarily to help members learn and benefit from their activities. Tour opportunities hold an enormous appeal for groups such as these.

Other groups may be primarily local, without an affiliation with similar organizations in other communities. Often, these groups focus on special projects that are unique to their town or city. Some examples would be the North port Boating Club, or the Seneca Valley Historical Society, or the Spruce Lake Theatrical Group. These are often closely knit organizations that might prefer a separate custom tour that includes sites and activities that are unique to their members.

Lastly, there are organizations that serve their members for special personal needs. Among these you will find support groups for members with traumatic problems - Alcoholics Anonymous, M.A.D.D., or AIDS awareness groups. Obviously, these groups will not usually be likely participants in your tour programs.

By examining the prospective client group possibilities, you now have a basis for determining the size and scope of future business. Of course, your financial limitations will be a guide to making reasonable basic decisions, such as whether the tours will be local, regional, domestic (within the U.S.) or international. It will also be a guide to the size of groups that can be served.

These are all considerations that are preliminary to establishing a group tour business. The more information you can gain, the better for a sound marketing plan. In addition, it would be wise to find out:

- What firms and organizations are currently offering tours in this area? (Request their brochures and follow their newspaper advertising.)
- What type, duration, and size of groups are involved in these tours?
- How frequently are these trips offered?
- How many years have these tour programs been offered?

- What age and interest groups make up their clientele?
- In the past several years, what, if any, tour firms have attempted to establish tour services but failed? What types of tours were offered? To what clientele?

From this information, we can conclude what competitors have already learned about tour opportunities in your area. We may think that we know this vicinity well, but we need some verified information now. A trip to the local Chamber of Commerce will help us to find out:

- What is the age distribution of the overall population (not in just this city, but in the area to be served?)
- What are the major occupations and income levels of the people?
- What are the general leisure and recreational interests of the residents? Do they change by season?
- What kinds of events "draw a crowd" in this area?

We have just gained some excellent guidelines for tour plans. Remember that we are creating experiences that are custom-made for the folks that we hope will become clients.

Of course if the company plans to serve customers in a larger area, perhaps even into adjacent states, the survey would bring in even more information. By storing all of these data into a computerized list, the operator has a sound, basic reference to use as he needs it.

Tour Groups as Clients

A group tour on the other hand, is scheduled to arrive at a specific destination for a declared activity. Participants will have similar accommodations and meals and will attend at least some of the same activities. They are together because they share an interest in the same destination, perhaps Tahiti and the Island in the Sun, The Calgary Stampede, or The

Royal Shakespeare Festival. Persons on the tour may be varied and quite different, but for this tour and this interval of time, these people have become an assembled group.

Open-Assembled Groups

The members of this tour group learned about the trip individually and chose to participate because of the desired experience. Not knowing more than one or two other members at the beginning didn't matter because the tour was their goal. But an interesting phenomenon occurs within these assembled groups. As the trip progresses, members continue to share experiences and discover many other mutual interests. Often, by the end of the tour, strong bonds and close friendships develop and some may become life-long friends.

Tour planners could be apprehensive about the types of features they should include for this group of varied individuals. After all, they have no idea what sorts of persons may purchase the trip. But they soon discover that the very nature and structure of the tour will tend to control the type of person who will be attracted to it.

• *The location and activities scheduled will need to be at least a marginal interest to the client. For example, a trip to Paris, including visits to Notre Dame, the Louvre and Versailles will automatically draw a somewhat informed person with at least a limited familiarity with history.*

Affiliated Groups

Fortunately, many groups who schedule tours already have many aspects in common among their members. As an organization or association, they have stated goals and purposes that draw people of similar professions or personal interests. Whatever their affiliations, these members have had occasions to share and assume the values of others in the group. They talk together easily, have mutual acquaintances, and have similar experiences to discuss and compare.

Sometimes the organized group originates the tour idea themselves even with specific destinations and preferred dates. They may contact a tour planner to arrange it for them. Or, they might search out an existing trip from a tour company and buy into it as a group.

The specified tour, scheduled at the group's choice of time and duration, becomes a custom group tour. The planner will need to coordinate arrangements carefully with the groups preferences, but it usually works out well. Occasionally, a custom tour for a small group can be expanded to be offered to other organizations with similar interests.

Planning with an established organization will have some advantages:

- Members are more likely to be motivated in signing up for a trip that relates to their special interests.
- Elected or appointed officers who represent the group.
- Unity and compatibility of the tour member is more likely to be developed.

It is always interesting to see that the affiliated group also experiences the same increased bonding that happens with the assembled tour group, and they value this strengthening aspect.

- Even the ages of the tour members may be somewhat controlled by the type of activities planned for the group.
- Lastly, the listed price will further limit the members' differences, simply because a certain percent of the population can't afford it financially.

So, even a general tour tends to draw those of somewhat similar interests, age levels and socio-economic groups. Tour organizers do realize that it is possible to shape a tour to be so limited in its appeal that it might not sell to capacity. For that reason, they wisely schedule some "on your own" special interests and activities.

Incentive Groups

The incentive tour is a special kind of trip that a company or business firm offers to its employees. The company pays for the tour which is a reward or recognition for its employees work performance. Usually, the tour is set up by the company representative and the tour operator with the details of the trip carefully planned.

By offering incentive travel, the company motivates their workers to sell or produce more, so the company benefits as well. It is good for employee morale and company loyalty as well. Usually incentive tours are not open to the public.

Other Kinds of Tours

Organizations or associations attending a convention or conference directed toward special interests often merge into touring groups. This may include clubs, societies, sports teams or artist groups. Their motivation may be a tournament, concert, geneological study or even a commemortive occasion and they wish to purchase a tour that is planned for their special requests and needs. They may require specific dates and times, as well as a certain destination, and expect their tour to be customized exactly to their standards. This type of tour is referred to as the custom tour.

Locating Clients For Group Tours

It may seem that selling tours is entirely the responsibility of a company's marketing division. It is true that they create the flyers, brochures and media promotions, but the actual contacts with buyers include many others in the firm. Tour planners are frequently the sales representatives, particularly when custom tours are concerned. Often, the escort staff will function as sales representatives as part of their work.

Questions for Further Study

1. Make a list of the organizations in your area that could become affiliated group clients.

2. What special interest groups could be contacted for tour possibilities? List types of tours that would be appropriate for each group.

3. To initiate some group travel considerations with your firm, write a sample "get acquainted letter" that you could send to an organization president.

SELECTING DESTINATIONS

One of your first decisions as tour planner is to decide where the group will go to get the most satisfaction from their trip. As you browse through travel literature, you might think that the possibilities are endless. But when you consider all of the variables at work in this plan, the number of choices becomes somewhat limited.

There is no simple formula to determine the right choices. Invariably, the decision will be based on the time, energy and money required to reach the location, and whether the experience can justify the investment. As in all consumer choices, we need to examine all of the alternatives.

Know Your Geography

As never before, you need information, and lots of it. If you have some courses and an interest in geography you have a good start. You have learned to read maps of countries, states, regions, and cities in areas where you might consider to travel. A good supply of maps is an excellent reference file. An up-to-date atlas will give you basic information but you should supplement that with detailed maps of specific states, regions and major cities. Large detailed maps can be obtained from auto clubs, auto service stations, and of course, from all tourist offices in states across the nation.

It takes practice and experience to read maps and understand all of the information they provide. Abbreviations and symbols may seem confusing at first, but they are excellent guides for the location that you are studying. You will even find distance scales on most maps, to help you plan travel segments. See Appendix #5 for some of the map symbols that you will be using.

Larger cities also distribute maps of their areas through their Chamber of Commerce or Visitor's Bureau. These are especially valuable for tour planners who need to know locations of airports, hotels, major attractions, and even their city bus and subway systems.

Larger cities distribute maps through their Chamber of Commerce or Visitor's bureau.

Studying geography will help you learn where the major countries of the world are located. You'll find out about their important cities, the language spoken, and the currency denominations. You also discover the location of fascinating sites such as:

- The Galapagos Islands
- The Great Barrier Reef
- Burchart Gardens
- Cascade Mountains
- Haleakala Volcano
- Mystic Seaport

You will learn where people can go to experience:

- whale watching
- dog sledding races
- white water rafting
- gold panning
- an outer space launching
- the best golf courses
- hot air balloon races
- horse races

And many other activities.

Available Services

Choosing a great place to go is easy, but it is not always simple to figure how to get there. That means convenient, affordable transportation so first we turn to our listings of airlines, railways and motorcoaches. Since your earlier tours will be shorter, less ambitious trips, you will probably restrict the distances you will consider. List all of the destinations you could visit within a one-, two- or three-day interval. List the popular attractions that are available in each of these areas. You may want to do the same for five- or seven- day trip possibilities.

Find out whether the trip will require several different carriers and transfers from one to the next. That could require a lot more time than it appears, perhaps even an overnight stay en route. It could be inconvenient, more expensive and frustrating to the travelers. A direct flight or a chartered bus trip might be a better possibility. Some destinations are just not easily accessible and that makes a difference in your planning.

You will also find out about the lodging and meals that are available in the area of the attraction. There should be a variety of convenient, reasonably priced services from which to choose.

Appropriate Activities

Study your brochures to learn as much as you can about the attraction itself. Does it require many hours of walking or standing? What admission fees are required? What are the various activities for option? Will the experience be worth the effort and cost of getting to the location?

Sometimes you can discover additional interesting sites in the area that will supplement the main attraction. They may not be spectacular, but they would add intrigue and more quality to the group's tour experience.

The acceptability of any destination depends heavily on the traveling group and their expectations. So, you will be considering their ages, agility and interests. Regardless of the flexibility you work into a tour plan, it usually results that a trip will have more appeal to one general age group. Teenagers and young adults will delight in an amusement park, a participation-type of sporting event or an early morning hot air balloon race. They won't complain if a departure is pre-dawn, the meals are all fast food or the return is late at night.

The acceptability
of any destination
depends heavily
on the traveling
group and their
expectations

But a more mature clientele has different expectations. Their satisfactions from tours often surround experiences they have read or heard about. Fantasy has convinced them that the sights and sensations of this long-awaited experience will be great. If they are in fairly good health, most adults (30 to 50 years) are ready and eager to go. They will ride through the wild animal safari park or a cable car across a canyon, with sheer delight and camera snapping. They will wander the trails in a botanical garden, climb the stairs of historic homes and explore for hours in a museum or art gallery. And most of them will return to the hotel, ready for a quick swim in the pool, followed by a four-course dinner and an evening at a lively night club.

Unfortunately, those energies begin to wind down with the years. By the time they retire, many folks have changed their expectations of tours. They still are eager to go, preferably not leaving before 7:30 a.m. Long periods of riding are tough, especially on arthritic bodies, so they need their journey to be reasonably short or in manageable segments. Meals are important for seniors who enjoy a hearty familiar menu, served promptly, with plenty of time for sitting and chatting afterward.

Activities planned for older people need to be somewhat controlled. Limited walking and standing time is a must. The total activity day needs to be shortened and flexible with optional events available for those who want them.

Sometimes you will schedule a tour that brings reservations from several different age groups. For example, the Ice Capades or a visit to Sea World has a universal appeal. Usually you can plan ways to coordinate the various needs of groups by allowing them to participate in situations with their peers. But generally, a child or two on an adult tour is unsettling and some older tour members even resent it.

There have recently been some interesting innovations in developing trips for grandparents to share with their grandchildren. Obviously these tours must be carefully planned to provide for the needs of both age levels. However, the concept is an interesting one and does offer a much needed solution for shared experiences for those family members. On the same scheme, many tour companies are experimenting with trips for families with destinations that parents and their children can enjoy together. It could be an excellent vacation alternative for families who deplore their limited quality time together.

From this time on you will be on a constant look-out for possible tour destinations. There is an abundance of suggested places in magazines and newspapers and televised programming. Your friends and relatives will describe events and places they have been. In fact, your own tour members may provide you with ideas. On your personal trips, you can often discover a place or activity that would become an appealing tour destination. But remember that you are selecting choices that attract your clients, and their needs and values may not always match with yours. An evening at the Grand Old Opry or a square dance festival may not "turn you on," but it could be a memorable event for your customers and a very profitable tour offering.

Resources For Information

Finding tour destinations would be an awesome job except that there are so many people who are ready and willing to help you. For example, each state government maintains a Department of Tourism staffed with knowledgeable, energetic persons. With multi-million dollar budgets, they produce colorful and appealing guides and brochures touting the features of their state. They recognize that their investment will bring in valuable revenues from conventions, tours and tour suppliers.

When you contact these offices in various states by phone

Professional Networking

or letter they will supply you with plenty of materials. You will read about state parks operations, festivals, celebrations, museums and special entertainment. Best of all, they have lists of hotels, restaurants and other suppliers along with contact names, addresses and phone numbers. As you look through these items you will begin to identify regions or areas within the state where there are a number of possible sites to visit. This is the beginning in your selection of destinations.

Each of these attractions usually has an access city within a reasonable driving distance. We tend to focus on these cities or towns because they will be more likely to have a wide variety of hotels and restaurants for your group's needs. In addition, the city usually has available resources for any possible emergency needs.

> **One of the best ways to learn about a destination is by contacting the Convention and Visitors Bureau in that city.**

One of the best ways to learn about a destination is by contacting the Convention and Visitors Bureau in that city. Their staff is employed specifically to promote tourism and they have a wealth of information to share with you. When you let them know that you are considering a tour to their vicinity, request a list of attractions, hotels, restaurants and a calendar of their upcoming events. You should also ask for a detailed city or area map which will be helpful. Very soon you will have another hefty supply of materials.

Already, you are realizing that tour planning must be done many weeks (indeed months) in advance of the tour. You will need to be working on spring and summer arrangements during the winter months to accomplish your task. It isn't always easy because some of the special events or seasonal rates are not fully scheduled. If you wait though, there may not be transportation available or enough rooms at your chosen hotel. Besides, early reservations usually get a better selection of seats at a performance, choice room locations and much better service from many suppliers. You can always change or even cancel a reservation if necessary, but at the last minute, you may have few alternatives.

As you search for information you will need to make numerous telephone calls. Use 800 numbers whenever possible to keep costs down. Always ask for the *group travel representative* who has pre-thought many of your concerns and even has information that you may not have considered. If you make a list of the questions you need to ask, you won't need to make repeat calls. Always give your name, company name and location when you indicate your interest in a tour to that area. Your name, incidentally, should be your first name. Find out your contact person's name and record it so you can reach him or her if you should call again. This saves time and helps you to start building a business link with him/her. Your contact person will probably give you his/her first name too. In travel communications, this is common practice. However, in written correspondence, you should use your full name.

By this time you have begun to narrow down the choices of possible suppliers, hotels, restaurants and such. You may feel fairly certain that you will follow through on your tour plans. But if you have not seen this destination recently, you will probably feel some uncertainty about your choices.

Familiarization Trips

Your better judgment guides you to invest the time and money to personally explore the destination. You can experience it all through the tour planner's eyes and be confident about your choices. This is your personal version of a familiarization trip. The travel industry has used this method for many years. Travel agents are offered low cost tours to areas where they are given opportunities to learn about various destinations. It is a promotional method by which agents can learn about new destinations and suppliers. It is an economical and educational experience for the travel agent who can help promote the services of the suppliers.

**Familiarization
trips are promo-
tional methods by
which agents can
learn about new
destinations and
suppliers.**

Supplier Contacts

But for you, this trip will become a learning tour. Each of the suppliers will be trying to encourage your bookings but your main purposes for this personal "fam" trip are to:

- provide you with a general perception of the area (the layout of the city or region and the location of places that will be featured in your tour).
- give you information about the real quality of the main attractions and activities (the setting, the related fees, and the ease of group participation).
- reveal how adequate your tentative choices are for hotels, restaurants, transfers, etc., and perhaps discover other better possible choices.
- determine information on time intervals required for moving a group from place to place during the segments of the tour.
- provide definite information regarding group rates and policies from each supplier being considered.
- become aware of possible problems or concerns that call for precautions or solutions.

Some well-organized desk-work is a must as you plan ahead for this trip. Schedule your appointments ahead with your various contacts so you make the most of your time there. If you study your city map, you can time your visits in one area and save shuttling around to see everyone. You might be wise to plan an early contact with the Convention and Visitors Bureau soon after you arrive. Sometimes they will offer to take you on a general tour of the city or area. But be sure to limit the time that would require. You have many places to go and people to see.

If you will need an overnight stay you may want to try one of your tentative hotel/motel choices. It is an excellent way to personally evaluate their services. Maybe you can also plan some meals at your tentative restaurants so you can see them in action.

In all of your conversations with the group tour representatives be sure to keep your questions and comments speculative. You won't be able to make final commitments until you have seen all of the possible choices. Besides, as long as you are undecided, the firms are more likely to be solicitous. They may even come up with better group prices of additional "perks" to make their offer more attractive to you. Always follow your pre-planned questions and record all of the information you are given. When you meet with so many persons in a short time, it is easy to become confused. See Appendix #6 for a suggested form for recording information about destinations and suppliers.

Leave each of your conferences with gracious, appreciative remarks and a promise to notify them about your plans when they are complete. Incidentally, you should be sure to send follow-up letters as a business courtesy.

Time Records

Throughout your trip you will need to envision just how it will be when you are directing a group of 40 or 50 people through this sequence. One big difference then will be the time you need to allow. The larger your group, the more time you will need.

You can hop on the subway or city bus by yourself and, watching for the correct stop, be off and at the museum entrance in a short 20 minutes. With a group, part of them may need to wait for the next bus or, heaven forbid, get off at the wrong stop. At that rate, your time can be doubled or tripled.

You can enter a restaurant by yourself, order a simple meal, be finished and paid for in less than an hour. A group, even with a pre-ordered menu choice, requires longer to serve, more time in the cashier's line, and of course, the usual time in the restroom. These are ways large groups function so we learn to deal with it.

Therefore, as you move from one segment of the trip to the next, timing is critical. Some events will be scheduled at a definite time so the transfer to get the group there on time must be carefully considered.

Even when your group is together on your chartered motorcoach remember that a drive will take longer than it would in your personal car. Buses are slower to maneuver in congested areas and entrances at events can be blocked by numerous other buses.

Set up a time index for each part of your trip. Record each interval that will affect your groups along with a few notes about special concerns. For example: from Regency Hotel to Sea World — 45 minutes, many stoplights after exit from freeway. Heavy traffic at noon and 5-6 p.m. (See Illustration 2 for a suggested form for recording necessary time intervals.)

Foreign Destinations

So far, we have concentrated on domestic tours, those within the United States. Most inexperienced tour planners don't try to arrange foreign group tours until they have more experience. As you can imagine, there are many more involved factors to consider with overseas tours. Here are a few of them:

Transportation

Foreign tours involve several, perhaps many, different segments of travel. Arrangements are necessary with air, land and maybe sea travel suppliers. Most of these are foreign-based airlines with widely differing reservation policies and procedures. Unless you are a certified travel agent you will need the assistance of a qualified agent. International airfares are complex especially when the trip includes a series of stopovers in various countries. In years ahead, you may want to attend a training program on international ticketing so you can handle these concerns on your own. In addition, there are varying regulations on baggage pieces, weights and on liability for damaged or lost luggage. These are all factors your certified travel agent can help you determine for the destination country(ies).

Time Differences

Time zones affect planning for domestic tours, but there are significant differences from continent to continent. Planning must include considerations about elapsed time throughout the trips. It also complicates activities in arrival areas when you are scheduling events for travelers who are affected by jet lag and fatigue. One difference in your schedule plan is the system which shows time on a 24-hour clock. Here, the timetable eliminates the use of a.m. and p.m. notation for hours of the day. Instead, the day begins at midnight, at 0000 to 0100 at 1:00 a.m. and on through the day. By 4:30 p.m., for example the time reads 0430.

Money Matters

In recent months, the exchange rate to some countries has been extremely volatile. This makes it difficult to negotiate prices for lodging, meals and ground transportation. It is entirely possible that an international tour planned six or nine months ago will suddenly cost much more in American dollars when the trip occurs. Even though the contracted agreement reads "specific number of U.S. Dollars" you may need to pay considerably more if the exchange rate has changed.

The same is true for members of a tour group, who may be disappointed when they exchange their U.S. dollars for foreign money. If you are involved in planning an international tour you would be wise to watch the exchange rates closely. They are listed in daily newspapers or you can inquire at your local bank. Other financial matters you will want to investigate include:

- Customs regulations and duty fees
- Special customs services for groups
- Additional city taxes on hotels/attractions

You will want to obtain a series of reference booklets available from:

> U.S. Customs Service
> Public Affairs Division
> 1301 Constitution Ave. N.W.
> Washington, D.C. 20229

Currencies are different in each foreign country and each has a different exchange rate.

Currencies are different in each foreign country and each one has an exchange rate as established by the United States and that country. So in each country our dollars equal a certain number of units of money, (eg., franc, peso, pound or krone, etc.). In fact, that exchange rate varies from day to day depending upon inflation rates and the value of the U.S. dollar in the world economics system.

To get information about the country you plan to visit, you need to contact the consulate or embassy which they maintain in the U.S. To obtain a directory to the foreign offices consulate contact:

> U.S. Printing Office
> N. Capital and H Street, N.W.
> Washington, D.C. 20401

These publications will also be helpful in providing information on legal regulations. People who travel to foreign countries, whether alone or in groups, must obtain permits to travel into and out of these nations. This involves passports, visas, (sometimes a tourist card) and citizens papers. Many countries also require immunizations against certain contagious diseases. All of this information is your responsibility as a tour planner. Each member of the tour group must be informed, so they can follow through with regulations.

Language and Social Practice

Arranging trips to a foreign country can be complicated if you are not familiar with terminology and practices there. You need to know for your own business procedures and also so you can inform your tour members about practical differences. Many of these guidelines involve subtle phrases or gestures that tourists may never imagine could be important. If a tour planner or escort has even limited knowledge of the language or culture of the country, he/she is fortunate.

Possible Solutions

Ideally, the tour planner would be able to make a personal advance trip to the country and experience all of these situations. However, this is financially impossible for most beginning independent tour operators. So, what are the alternatives?

- You could arrange for your group to purchase a block of reservations from an established tour operator who has a trip already scheduled to that country or region. With diligent searching, you can locate a reliable operator with a trip that is similar, or at least adaptable, to the needs of your group.
- You may be able to make most of your arrangements through a group operator in each of the cities/countries where you plan to go. That contact person must be an experienced and well-recommended travel professional who can help you locate the suppliers you will be

needing for the tour. Of course, they will be charging a fee or commission, so this will add to the cost of your tour. Those contact persons are listed with that country's tourist office in major American cities.

This arrangement requires that you can stay in close communication with that group operator throughout the planning. It isn't the easiest way to plan foreign tours, but it does accomplish the task.

Periodically, familiarization trips are offered to foreign countries by international suppliers and tourism offices. They often do not include the specific destination you are concerned about but you could learn a great deal about conditions and services in that country. These low-priced excursions are an excellent way to explore new areas for future tours. Available fam trips are publicized in trade journals and papers of the travel industry. You may want to watch for their announcements and take advantage of the opportunities.

Trends in Foreign Travel

International unrest has taken a devastating toll on the travel industry. Rising fuel prices affect transportation cost which, in turn, are reflected in our prices. Leisure travel is the first to feel the impact of wartime conditions and as hostilities intensify, business and other necessary trips abroad are also restricted.

Meanwhile, the shrinking dollar in the international market is making profitable tours to other countries nearly impossible. Clients take a dim view of a tour that carries warnings of terrorism, airport security delays and much higher costs. Even cruise lines are feeling the pinch from travelers who avoid the flight segment on their air-sea packages.

These factors, along with the recession conditions that currently plague our country, do not encourage international tour projects. In fact, a more profitable approach may be toward tours for inbound tourists (those who are visiting from other countries). Recent years have brought millions of inbound tourists to our country and the trend continues.

Whether their groups seek shopping tours in cities or scenic tours of our natural and historic sites, they will benefit from well-directed tours.

It is not easy to be optimistic about business futures during an international crisis. Perhaps this time is best used to reconsider the best routes to new types of domestic tours that are practical and fill a demand. Many operators are concentrating on shorter, more frequent trips to maintain their volume. Others are innovating some special interest features that will attract more clientele. Whatever develops, we all hope for an early end to these crises and a rapid recovery from their effects. Interest in travel and tourism will continue to thrive as it always has.

Questions for Further Study

1. Name 3 destinations that would offer appealing activities for teenagers and young adults.

2. Make a list of the types of activities that would be appropriate for people of retirement age.

3. What time is it now by the 24 hour clock?
   What time will you eat dinner?
   What time will you go to bed?

PRICES & PROFITS

It's easy to understand why group tours have become so popular. They are an excellent value for the price. The reason they can be offered for these prices is because suppliers offer discounts for group sales. And the larger the group, the more likely that the group discount will be significant.

Suppliers, like all other businesses, are eager to increase the volume of their sales. In order to attain full capacity in seating and lodging or audience services, management can afford to accept a reduced price for a volume sale of tickets.

This is a common practice in merchandising. We all know that buying a case of items will mean that you pay a lower price per unit. But it is even more important with travel and hospitality suppliers because they are not dealing in tangible merchandise. They have a set number of seats on a plane or bus, rooms in a hotel, or seats in a theater. Their operating costs remain the same whether two or 50 use the service. So, their answer is "Go for the 50…better yet, 250."

When suppliers set their prices for a season or event, they have to realize that there will be occasions when all of the space isn't filled. Their final price decision must allow for that possibility. Therefore, the published price will be somewhat higher to allow for those low days. They may offer special priced promotions for the dates when sales usually lag behind or they might advertise an attractive package sale that would draw more buyers. The fact is that suppliers do allow some price margins for possible discounts and it is an effective management strategy.

When you realize that prices for services can be negotiated, you will become a part of the process. You will be watching for opportunities to benefit from group discounts each time you contact a supplier. As a tour operator, you will be using these same methods as you set your tour prices and try to estimate your profits. Remember to search out every possible supplier before you decide to sign up for a service. If there are only two or three choices it will be easy, but often there are many. Know enough about each one so you can make a smart comparison.

Prices for services can and should be negotiated.

Follow these guidelines as you reach your decisions:

- Avoid early commitments that may bind you until you are really sure but keep in mind that waiting too long may cause you to lose out entirely.
- Try to arrange all reservations by unit (eg., 38 persons @ $35.00 each instead of a service for a "block" of seats or a charter that can handle 100 people). When you buy a charter service your price is the same regardless of the number of participants.
- Always determine how many seats from your original reservation you can vary without penalty.
- Always check each contract to be certain of the amount and date of a deposit. Also find out if the deposit is refundable in case you would need to cancel the tour.

Policies such as these are usually firmly established by each firm. Even though they seem congenial and flexible during discussions and planning, the agreement on the contract is the one the firm is likely to use. Any special policy arrangements should be in writing.

The best way to learn costing and pricing for tours is to personally experience it. Let's start out with an uncomplicated one-day trip. This will be offered to the public, so it becomes an assembled group tour.

Many baseball fans in your town are excited about the outcome of the World Series this season. You have decided to schedule a group tour to the championship game. It will be played on October 18 at 1:30 p.m., at Metro Stadium in Major City, U.S.A. (about 150 miles from your town).

This should be fairly simple…

- Obtain tickets for the number of persons going.
- Arrange transportation for the group.
- Plan for meals, if any will be necessary.
- Figure the cost per person for the trip.
- Determine the price that you will need to charge.

A Case Study…
A Simple
One-Day Excursion

FIRST PRIORITY…Event Tickets

Scheduling entertainment for a group means buying admissions for a specific number of people for a certain event. Some events managers offer group discounts, others have varied prices relative to seating location, and yet others schedule a season price (a sort of package price for a number of performances). For a high demand event like the World Series there are not usually group discounts available. However, seats in a good location will be purchased early so you will need to obtain your tickets early. Remember, you have not even announced the trip yet so you will need to estimate the number of tour participants you will have. These are nonrefundable tickets, so any that are unsold will be a loss against the tour.

Decision… You decide to take a chance on 40 tickets
@ $22 each.

Let's Take It
Step By Step…

SECOND PRIORITY...Transportation

If you have direct flights available from your town to Major city, the flight alone will take about an hour. However, you'll need to get your group from the airport to Metro stadium and back—perhaps at times when thousands of fans will be needing the same service so traffic will be heavy.

Your best round trip flight to Major City is $62, the group rate. Transfer bus rates are $7.50 per person, each way for a total of $15. Add $15 and the round trip flight totals $77.

Let's consider the train. If there are convenient train schedules to Major City you could arrange for the group to travel by rail. Their round trip group rate is only $51. Or course, they will still need transfers from the train station to the stadium, and return, as before. Add $15 and the rail trip totals $65.

Now let's consider a motor coach alternative. The trip will take more time but the bus can provide both services. Instead of round trip and transfers, it can travel directly to the stadium. Maybe it won't require that much more time, after all. The cost to charter a motorcoach with a capacity of at least 40 is $955.00. If 40 people are going, the cost per person will be only $23.00. Of course it will be proportionately higher if fewer people go. For example, with 30 passengers it is $35.00 each, with 20, it rises to $48.00. Finally, at lower numbers the price becomes nearly equal to air or rail costs. Chartered service is economical but only for assured large groups. Of course, you can't predict the response to your tour publicity so your only solution is vigorous marketing to fill your tour.

Disadvantages of the bus are the longer riding period and limited mobility during the trip. Advantages are the direct and convenient access to the event. You will take all of these factors into consideration. Since the game is the prime importance here, most people will be attracted to the trip that is convenient, safe, and economical.

Decision...you choose the motor coach at $23.00 per person.

> **Most people are attracted to a trip that is convenient, safe and economical.**

THIRD PRIORITY...Meals

When a trip extends through more than five or six hours we need to consider the meals that may be necessary. With an air tour that is scheduled at 1:30 p.m. passengers might be able to depart after an early lunch and return before dinner time if the flight times are convenient. But with the slower trip by rail or bus, both lunch and dinner will probably need to be considered.

On many short trips, meals are simply not included in the price of the tour. Instead, you need to plan stops where passengers can purchase food. A lunch or dinner stop at a fast food restaurant will often be adequate for a bus load of passengers. However, this doesn't remove your responsibility as a tour manager. The restaurant needs to know of your intended arrival time and the approximate size of the group otherwise you may be faced with a 40-minute wait while other scheduled groups are served.

On many short trips, meals are not included in the price of the tour.

Included Meals

If you do decide to include a meal on this tour, it needs to be pre-arranged with the restaurant (group manager). In the interest of convenience and saving time you may prefer to select a cafeteria or buffet where individual choices won't be a problem. Other times, you might choose a single entree meal, usually their well-known specialty (eg., fried chicken meals or barbecued rib dinners). These arrangements are often offered with a group discount as well as free meals for the tour director and driver.

Prices for included meals vary so much that you would need to discuss them in advance and decide whether that particular group would value it enough to include it.

Decision...Let's say that meal stops for this trip will be arranged for "on their own" lunches and suppers.

Estimating Tour Prices

At this point, we have made decisions so we can figure the price that must be charged for each passenger:

```
Transportation: Motor coach ....................... $995.00
Event tickets: 40 @ $22.00 each ................... 880.00
Add any other expenses you will have:
Flyers and brochures for publicity .................. 60.00
Candy treats for passengers, en route ............... 6.00
Courtesy tip for the bus driver ....................... 25.00
total costs ...................................................... 2,036.00
divided by 40 .................................... $51.00 per person
```

Now, you must add your mark-up to make sure you have a profit:

```
add 30% ................................................. 15.30 per person
price of the tour ................................... 66.30 per person
```

Since this is an odd amount, you might round it off at $65.00 or at $67.50, but it shouldn't vary much from that figure. If you take 40 passengers your profit will be $612.00 (40 x $15.30). But remember, for each person less than 40 your profit will be reduced by $56.00. In fact, if you have 11 empty seats, your profit will be zero. This is what is referred to as the break-even point. So, you see the importance of vigorous marketing at all times. If you feel that you need a larger margin, you have to increase the tour price accordingly, as much as you think the clientele will accept.

A Case Study... A Five Day Trip

Now let's consider the factors involved in a multi-day trip. Your tour business in Case City has been asked to plan a convention tour for a local organization of business women. Their chapter of 150 members is a strong, active group celebrating their 50th anniversary of professional and community service this year . They plan for at least 35 members to participate in their national meeting in Denver, Colorado (700 miles away). The convention opens with a dinner meeting on Thursday, June 26 and closes Saturday, June 28 at 3:30 p.m. The group would like to extend their tour for a couple of days to enjoy the sight of Denver and the surrounding area if it doesn't add too much extra cost to the tour.

You decide to plan a five-day trip for June 26-30.

Transportation

Now, we have several types of transportation needs:

a. A round trip from Case City to Denver and return

b. Transportation within the city of Denver

c. Sightseeing travel in the area

Again, consider all of the possibilities:

a. Airline - Unfortunately, there is no direct flight available from Case City to Denver. The group will need a flight segment to Hub City and second segment on to Denver. Even with convenient connections this will require more time and cost. After checking with the airlines group reservationists you find the best price for the round trip to Denver is $256.00 per person. (If it were a large group, it might be feasible to charter a plane for a direct flight for your group but with only 35 persons the price would be prohibitive.)

b. Transportation within the city of Denver - After arrival at the airport, transfer is needed to and from the hotel (about $6.50 per person), numerous trips for the group from their hotel to the convention center (these will vary depending upon location of hotel), and a guided city tour (requested by the group - $12.50 each).

c. Sight-seeing outside of the city - A full day scenic mountain tour is available at $27.50 per person, group rate.

Consider all other means of transportation:

Railway - There is no train connection available from Case City to Denver, so this possibility is not considered.

Motorcoach - Prices vary among the three companies you have contacted. The best price quoted was a 1 week charter for $3,995.00. With 35 passengers, this will cost about $135.00 per person for the round trip and throughout the 7 days.

The time is significantly more by bus, probably requiring a two- to three-day trip each way to and from Denver. This, in turn, requires an overnight in a hotel/motel and extra meals each way en route. However, the bus and driver will be available all week for city and sight-seeing access so that will be a savings. A bus charter for the trip will probably require seven days. The total cost will depend upon how many meals and overnights you include in the price of the tour.

Making a decision on transportation

Now it is time to "sharpen your pencil" and balance out the calculations. Provide your figures to the group leader so their preferences will guide your decision. The two extra days on the road may seem too long to them, especially if it doesn't offer some impressive scenic areas or interesting overnight locations. Remember that time may be a premium to these business women and they may be unwilling to include two extra days. On the other hand, if any of them have anxieties about flying, that could sway some of the group from the airlines decision. Just be sure that you have definite price figures along with the list of included features for **each alternative** in order for the group to react to your suggestions.

Lodging Accommodations

Your research on hotels was helpful and you came up with the three best choices:

Hotel X - an older, well established hotel, remodeled and attractive, located within walking distance of the convention center. The group rate offered was $34.00 per person, double occupancy, per night.

Hotel Y - A newer, more elegant building also located within easy access of the convention center. The group rate here is higher at $44.00 per person.

Hotel Z - a beautiful hotel, located about four miles from the downtown area. It is adjacent to a lovely recreation area, complete with tennis courts, pools, and even a dinner theater. A mountain view and escape from city confusion make this an appealing alternative. Group rate is $47.00 per person.

All three hotels offer the basic in-room amenities and do have nonsmoking rooms upon request. All have attached restaurants and lounges. Basic service is the same for all of them.

Make your decision:

As before, you will need to determine the preferences of your group before you make final decisions. Consider that hotels X and Y are close to the convention center, eliminating daily taxi and bus fares. Your group may be elated with the idea of the recreation activities at Hotel Z but they may also see it as an unnecessary expense as they will be mainly focused on convention activities. This is a custom tour, so the group's choices are important.

Attractions & Entertainment

Meanwhile, you have been planning the activities that can be included to enhance the group's enjoyment of their additional tour days. You have searched out availability and prices for:

- a general city tour, soon after their arrival in Denver.
- special attractions, museums, art institutes, historic sites.
- performance events that will be scheduled on those dates.

With such limited time to fill, you need to select one or two of these that would be especially appealing. Determine the prices and decide whether these will be included in the price of the tour. As an alternative, you could list some as optional activities for members to do on their own.

Since the group specified some sight-seeing outside the city in the surrounding area, you need to schedule the side trip and determine the price per person. Thats need to be included in the tour price although it could be optional if the group agrees.

Meals & Refreshments

These arrangements will not be such a major decision on this tour since so much time will be devoted to convention activities. Meals will fit into meeting schedules and personal plans. In this case, the meals you need to arrange will be:

- Breakfasts each morning (provided by restaurants in the hotel). These can be continental breakfasts or planned single menus each day. You will need to reserve and prearrange these with the hotel restaurant manager.
- Dinner on the evening after the convention closes. (This could be a good time to schedule a special event such as a dinner theater or a meal at a prestigious restaurant.)
- Lunch on the all day sight-seeing trip. (Sometimes the meal is included by the tour company operating the side trip. In this case it is not, so you will need to make arrangements with a restaurant in advance.) Dinner on Sunday evening is not included. (On their own)

Costing The Entire Trip

Finally, with all of this information and definite prices to use, decisions can fall into place. Now it is time to assemble all of the prices of included features, by categories, into a cost plan. It will probably look something like this:

Transportation: per person
Airline Round trip to Denver $256.00
City tour 12.00
Mountain view sight-seeing tour 27.50
Total **$296.00**

We avoided the cost for transfers from the airport to hotel by scheduling the use of the hotel courtesy van. It may require a little more time, but it is a significant savings. By choosing a hotel within walking distance of the convention center the tour members will have no taxi or bus costs.

Accommodations: Hotel X: 18 double rooms @ $68.00 per night (Complimentary room for tour director nights @ $34.00 per night)
Per person $136.00
Baggage handling
Arrival & departure @ $2.00 ea. 4.00
Total **$140.00**

Meals: Breakfasts were negotiated with the hotel to be continental breakfasts (juice, rolls, coffee) as part of the room price. There is no additional cost.

Dinner on Saturday was included in the cost of dinner theater entertainment. Again, there was no additional cost.
Lunch on the Sunday sightseeing tour $6.00
Dinner Sunday evening is "on their own."
Lunch on Monday will be an in-flight meal
Total meals .... **$6.00 ea.**

Meal expenses are often a major cost on a tour. In this case situation, we have tried to include meal charges along with other negotiated costs. It is not usually possible to arrange this many meals into other tour costs. But it does show you some ways to reduce meal charges. We are actually doing a bit of packaging within the tour plan.

Entertainment:
Sightseeing costs have already been listed under transportation. The major cost for entertainment was for the dinner theater performance.

Total .... $23.00 ea.

Summary of costs per person
Transportation $296.00
Accommodations 140.00
Meals 6.00
Entertainment 23.00
Total $465.00

Now we have a tour cost per person. It's a pretty decent price for a tour that includes so much. But now we realize that there are other expenses related to tour planning. These are hidden costs and they are often easy to disregard but they do add up and need to be included.

Check out the hidden costs:
Flyers prepared for publicity $8.50
Mailing costs 38.60
Phone calls 21.18
Incidentals, such as tips, tolls and occasional
on-board treats for the group 7.00
Total hidden cost is $75.28

Divide this amount by the
number of your members: 35 .... $2.15
Add it to your previous cost figure 465.00
Total cost for each person $467.15

Don't forget to add your mark-up to ensure your profit on the tour. In this case let's make it 27.5% or $128.47 per person. Round the number to an even figure and the final tour price will be $595 per person. This plan and price will bring you a profit of $128.50 on each sold reservation. If all 35 persons decide to go, your profit will be $4497.50.

However, as with the previous case study, if you only sell 30 reservations (or maybe even less) you will need to subtract accordingly from your profits. We were wise to avoid any chartered or blocked reservations on this trip. Even so, many group discount prices are not applicable, when the size of the group goes below a certain number. Keep these things in mind when you are marketing your tour.

There is always the possibility that the group may view your plan as simply too costly. In that case, they could lose interest or abandon their plans. You need to pre-think that possibility and have some alternatives ready to suggest. For example:

- The entire trip by motor coach would be much less expensive if the group could accept the two extra days of necessary travel time.
- A less expensive hotel can be suggested perhaps not with all of the special amenities but clean, comfortable, safe and pleasant.
- Entertainment and sight-seeing tours can be limited to lower cost and no-admission activities which are often delightful experiences.

Cutting Costs On Tours

**Negotiate with
suppliers for the
best group prices**

- Fewer meals can be included in the tour price and less expensive restaurants can be chosen.

Much of your success in obtaining significant group discounts depends upon your ability to negotiate with suppliers. This is a process of discussion about the needs you have for their services and the terms that they can reasonably offer. This is not a bickering procedure but a method of sharing information at a professional level.

As a tour operator, you will share in negotiations. Sometimes it takes place by telephone or by letters but it often occurs in-person when you meet with suppliers as you do on fam trip. Here are some suggestions for your negotiations. Start out by doing some homework in preparation for the discussion.

You need to introduce yourself, describe the kind of tour business you are operating, and the concerns you need to discuss. Even though you have made an appointment, your group service representative may not have the necessary information for your session.

- In a brief statement describe the tour group, size, and focus of the tour along with the dates of your visit.
- Conclude with a general statement about the service you need specifying the dates and times. Complete information is basic to a cooperative discussion such as this.
- Indicate that you are searching for the optimum service for the best price. (At this point, your choices are tentative. If they believe that you are ready to reserve with them they will more likely offer their standard group price and leave the acceptance up to you.)
- If they respond that your basic minimum requirements cannot be provided (eg., no rooms available on those dates) you have no need to pursue the discussion further.
- If they can provide your minimum requirements, then find out more detail about their services. (Do they offer

no-smoking rooms? Is baggage handling provided? etc.) At this point the supplier is trying to prove their adequacy for your needs so they volunteer further enticements for your group.

- As you inquire about group prices, follow their response with an inquiry about what is included for that price.
- Meanwhile, record all information. Their statement of rates does not bring an elated response from you. Simply record it and study your figures thoughtfully.
- Now, question further about other services offered (eg. a complimentary continental breakfast? A welcome reception for the group?). Your contact person will respect your concern for details and completeness of your planning.
- Ask for policies on deposits, full payments, cancellations, etc. Be sure to find out about penalties for irregular procedures. Record all information in detail.
- When you have all necessary information, express your gratitude for their help and close the conference with your intent to contact them with your decision. Be sure to follow through as you promised.

Negotiation conferences are not only excellent means of arranging business deals, but they are also a way to develop a network of professional contacts.

Negotiation conferences are excellent means of arranging business deals. They are also a good way to develop a network of professional contacts. You may be impressed at the many original and innovative ideas they may share with you.

All this negotiating and deliberating has hopefully brought about an agreement on the kind of services you hope to arrange. As you discussed the various aspects of the plan there was the usual head nodding and verbal commitment. Even though it concluded with a handshake, all you have, so far is an agreement.

Agreements & Contracts

Every business transaction needs to have some verification, hence a saleslip, when you purchase an item. In this case, you are arranging for services to be performed at a future date. Weeks, perhaps even months will pass before that time comes. Without a legal commitment you have only personal trust to rely on. Therefore we rely on the most important tool of our trade: a contract.

A contract is a powerful device that serves as a safety net for both you (the buyer) and the supplier (the seller). It is legally binding and clarifies the details of the business deal. A well-prepared contract specifies:

> **A contract is a powerful device that serves as a safety net**

- the buyer, the supplier and the business firms they represent
- a complete description of the services to be performed and for a specified number of people
- dates and times of service
- specific details regarding the performed service
- required participation by buyer (eg. group member names for room assignments)
- required dates for final numbers to be served
- dates for deposit if required
- provision for refunds, cancellations, adaptation of dates
- exact figures on prices, taxes and service fees.
- payment terms and procedure
- penalties in violation of contract

These provide the ground rules for a sound business agreement. When each party has a copy of the contract, it can be used for reference and to verify your plans. Most of the time, responsible parties will fulfill the provisions as they were set up. But, if for any reason the terms were violated, the printed and signed document is valid, even if taken into court.

As a tour planner, you have the responsibility to make certain that the details of a contract are clear and workable.

It should ensure you a planned service will be done as you requested it. It also outlines certain provisions for you to carry out, and you are legally responsible for them.

Remember...a signed contract means business.

Now, it's your turn:

Set up a one-day trip for 40 persons to attend a dinner theater presentation in a city that is 75 miles away. It is an evening show begining at 6:00 p.m. and ending at 10:15 p.m. There is no train or air service to that city, so the transportation will need to be by motor coach.

- Charter cost: $915.00
- Dinner theater tickets are $24.00 each

What price will you need to charge per person?

How much profit will you realize if you have only 26 persons attending, instead of 40?

What contracts will you need to arrange and sign for this trip to be completed?

Activity For Further Study

RECORD KEEPING

CHAPTER EIGHT

At first glance, a career in tour management might seem to be fairly stress-free. It is, after all, a profession that centers on pleasure trips for groups of people. What could possibly cause anxiety or strain?

But remember the old adage "Nothing really wonderful just happens, someone had to plan for it." This is particularly true of tours. This is work that involves a series of scheduled events and many participants with an orderly plan, that will fulfill everyone's expectations. But with one broken link in the chain of events, get ready for chaos.

Basically this is work that involves a series of scheduled events and many people who are going to help make it happen, as well as hosts of clients who are expecting to participate. As we plan, negotiate, sell, and conduct the tour, each day is filled with concerns you will need to recall or refer to. In the busy whirl of getting all arrangements made, we are tempted to believe that we'll remember details. But the human mind simply cannot catalog and retain so much information. In fact, by the time the actual tour takes place, much of your information can become blurred.

All businesses need to set up systems for record-keeping if for no other reason than to monitor profits and to report taxes. Even more than other companies, tour businesses demand considerable paper work in all aspects of their operations. If you are employed by a tour company, they will undoubtedly have bookkeeping and accounting departments who will be maintaining balance sheets on your tours. In addition, you will have lots of other information that you will need to refer to and work with every day.

Fortunately, your computer system will simplify most of these records for you. If you can make simple entries and retrieve data that you will need again, it will certainly be helpful. Those who work with large firms will discover that they have well-designed spread sheets that will condense information so it will be ready. Of course, if you are operating independently it will be your job to set up these systems on your own.

Clientele Records

One of the most important files you will maintain is your customers lists. These are critical for your marketing efforts in promoting your tours.

Group Data Forms

Set aside one section of your clientele file for organizations and agencies in your city or sales area. These are the affiliated groups who can become your clients for custom tours. You need a list of these groups along with the names, addresses and phone number for the contact person of each. The form should also provide space for you to enter memos about your contacts with them.

Here is a suggested group data form:

If you have access to a computer it will be easy to set up an accumulative record on groups that are prospective customers. An ordinary card file would serve the purpose just as well if you have no computer available.

Organization	Contact Person	Address	Phone
AARP	Joe Wilson	345 Maple St. Centerville, TX	555-1234
Date	**Activity**	**Memo**	
2/15	Initial Contact	General interest - left brochure	
2/27	Joe called for appointment	Group interested - convention tour	
3/4	Appt. w/ Joe & travel chair.	Obtained details on tour plans	
3/11	Appt. with Joe	Presented tentative tour	

Customer Lists

The other section of your client file should be made into a complete customer list. These are the names of persons who have traveled with your tours or who have indicated an interest in future tours. Again, a computer list will be quickly accessible for mailing labels or for reference purposes. A card file may take a bit longer to assemble but will serve equally as well.

Of course, these files should be kept up-to-date so the information continues to be useful.

Name	Address	Phone
Alice Jones	608 South St. Centerville	555-1221
Memo Went on the fall color tour to Smokies. Interested in Las Vegas trip in February.		

Tour Records

You will discover that each tour is unique in the way it operates and in specific details. It is important to keep careful notations on every trip. These are your working records and they include several types of information. You will soon learn that you need a separate file folder for each tour. It works best to use a multi-pocketed folder to handle each of the types of records involved. Most companies assign an identification number or code to each tour so they can clearly differentiate between the various trips. You may wish to do that, also.

Supplier Negotiations

One section of the tour records must provide a log with every contact and communication that you have with suppliers for that tour. Set up the file so you can use it throughout your planning and marketing periods.

At any one moment you should be able to know from your records:

Because every tour is unique in the way it operates and in specific details, it is important to keep careful notations on every trip.

- What negotiations have taken place and with which contact person
- Any agreements concluded
- All contracts confirmed and signed
- All deposit and payment deadlines
- Cancellation deadlines

(See Appendix #8 for a suggested record form.)

Tour Itinerary

As you complete the tour plan it should be finalized with an itinerary. This is an hour-by-hour (sometimes minute-to-minute) schedule that your tour group will follow. Copies of the itinerary should be made for each staff person who will be participating: tour director, escort, motorcoach dispatcher/ driver, and even step-on guides or hosts. When everyone has the necessary information, cooperation is greatly improved.

Promotion Materials

By this time, the marketing department has launched their plans for selling the tour. It may be a part of a brochure listing all of this season's tour offerings, a separate flyer that promotes a single tour or a newspaper or magazine advertisement. Whatever the effort, copies of these should be filed with your tour records.

Passenger Lists

As reservations begin to come in you will need to set up a passenger list. This will help you to check on the total numbers as they near capacity. You will also use it for hotel rooming lists, luggage and name tags, and for pre-tour communications. (See Appendix #9 for a passenger list form.)

Financial Records

You need to record all receipts and disbursements in your company ledger. You may frequently have checks coming in from more than one tour at the same time. Keep separate income and payout records for each tour to stay ahead of the deadlines and penalties. (See Appendix #10 for suggested financial records form.)

Record ALL receipts and disbursements.

Balance Sheet

When the tour is over and all of the commitments are paid it is time to assemble a final summary on financial matters relative to that tour. This final statement is the balance sheet. (Refer to Appendix #11 for a suggested form for this final report.)

Even though the tour records are now complete and this file is labeled as "inactive," this is an extremely valuable resource. Although you may never repeat this exact tour, you have a wealth of information that you can use for a similar or adapted tour. It may save you considerable time and effort. File your inactive tour folders where they can be retrieved for just that purpose.

Marketing Records

Bookkeeping System

We have already discussed the need for a company bookkeeping procedure. By maintaining accurate records of receipts and disbursements it is possible to know the status of your business at all times. Best of all, it becomes the basis for your decisions on future ventures. Incidentally, when the annual auditing time rolls around, your financial records will be in good shape.

Hidden Costs

In Chapter 7 we referred to the often-ignored tour costs that need to be subtracted from the profits on a tour. These hidden costs are very much a part of operating a business. They include: toll charges on long distance telephone calls, office supplies and equipment, and automobile expenses related to the tour business.

Additionally, if you are leasing office space this is a significant cost. You will need to develop record keeping methods for each of these hidden costs. It may be a mileage diary that you keep in your car to record various errands or you may keep a separate ledger for operations. Whatever your method, you will need to set up some workable routine for recording these expenses.

Promotional Costs

Every business has to invest some of their funds in continually improving their visibility and customer support. These promotional costs are quite varied. Some of them are general and promote your total tour business, (eg. a seasonal brochure, an advertising space in the yellow pages, or a tour display at the local summer holiday fair). These costs do mount up so you should keep accurate records of them.

Other promotions are related to a specific tour. When you design, duplicate, and mail out flyers for a trip, that cost is a definite debit against the tour budget. You need to designate those costs in your ledger so they will be appropriately charged.

Office routines such as record keeping are often easy to postpone, especially when you are in the midst of some urgent tour preparations. Some people deal with that problem by scheduling a specific two or three hour interval each week, restricting that time to record keeping. Whatever method you use, maintain your records with care. Be sure that your co-workers are abiding by the same system, whether it is computerized or manual.

1. What are the possible consequences of the following neglected records?

   a. No recorded deadline dates for a deposit for the hotel?

   b. Not all customers have been recorded on passenger lists at a given time?

   c. Cancellation was made after the deadline date for the motorcoach company?

2. Name five hidden costs that a tour director must be certain to record.

Questions For Further Study

THE TOUR ITINERARY

By this time you realize that a quality tour is not planned in a day...or even a week. It is shaped up gradually as each of the components is arranged with the various suppliers. In some ways a tour is much like a theatrical production with you, as the director, fitting together all of the "acts" into a smoothly running sequence. But in this case, the script is written at the end of all of the planning.

The "script" for a tour is the day-by-day or, better yet, the hour-by-hour plan called an itinerary. It helps to visualize how each segment will occur and the best way to move from each activity to the next one. The following is an example of the kind of planning that is important for the itinerary:

In order to reserve a group dinner at a restaurant you need to figure what time the group would be departing from their previous event or activity. Then, you estimate how long it will take to transfer the group to the restaurant. We all do this kind of time planning in our daily lives and it is easy with only one or a few persons. If you arrive a little late or early, it's no big problem, the irregularity is usually overlooked. However, if your reservation is for 40 or 50 people, special arrangements have been made by the restaurant. Extra waiters may have been assigned and expensive quantities of food are prepared. A delay can become a serious problem.

A long delay for a group reservation may even cause it to be canceled and your problem may become a crisis. You don't even want to think about the attitude changes in your disappointed, hungry tour members. Give high priority to making practical and workable schedules that fit into the time intervals between major events.

Placement of Main Features of the Tour

As a tour planner, you have already been forced to choose times for the main features to be included in the tour. Some of them were obvious:

- Arrival and check-in at a hotel/motel which naturally follow when you reach your destination city.
- Many of the special events are already scheduled and publicized and, of course, cannot be changed.
- Many other attractions have established "open" hours and sometimes limits on days of operation.

So, you arrange your schedule around the main features that have set performance times. Here are some helpful guidelines you might follow:

- If possible, do not schedule a major event immediately following a long tiring trip by plane, train or bus.
- Plan special tour events several hours or even days apart so the tour members can enjoy each one fully.
- Fill in the blocks of time between interesting related activities that can be flexibly arranged.
- On longer tours, use "on their own" intervals occasionally to cushion against deadline pressures and too much togetherness.

Tour participants seem to value major attractions more if they have time ahead to anticipate, a leisurely arrival and departure and time afterward to savor the experience and discuss it with their companions. Crowding in more activities does not necessarily mean that tour members get more for their tour price. It may add schedule problems for you and, very likely, more stress and fatigue for participants. Consider time as a resource to be invested wisely in the most rewarding intervals you can include.

When we set departure times for our groups, we tend to estimate the necessary lead time from the printed schedule and our own experience in boarding a plane or bus. Your flight information indicates that the plane will depart at 2:15 p.m. You know that boarding will begin about 2:00 p.m., so your group should arrive at the terminal by 1:15 p.m. to check in their luggage and go the gate area by 1:45 p.m. **WRONG!** Do you know how long it takes to check in 40 people and their luggage? Or how long it takes them to get through security check these days? Or for you to survey the arrivals to be sure that have all reached the gate area?

The time required for a group to move through a series of activities is unpredictable, but it is nearly always much longer than you would expect. Besides, one of lifes realities is that a certain small percentage of people are habitual deadline pushers. You can urge them to be prompt but you might better accept the futility of changing these folks and advance the time for them to arrive at the terminal. Give yourself the luxury of an extra half hour at least. Set the time at 12:45 p.m. for a comfortable margin.

The same is true of charter bus departures for your groups. Although the check-in and luggage loading may move more quickly, you will still want to allow for irregularities that are time consuming.

Speaking of departures, it is important that you clearly specify the location where the group will assemble before

Crowding in more activities does not necessarily mean that tour members get more for their tour price.

Consider time as a resource to be invested wisely in the most rewarding intervals you can include.

they leave. In your pre-tour instructions this should be clearly stated and emphasized ("at the information desk on the second level in the main terminal at Metro Airport"). Follow that same rule whenever you are assembling or reassembling your tour group, to carefully specify the location and time.

When you arrive at your destination/airport, a scheduled bus should be waiting to take your group to the resort where they will be staying. But even the baggage claim and boarding the bus requires more time than you had expected. You arrived at 3:55 p.m., but by the time your group has boarded the bus it is 4:20 p.m. The bus heads out into the evening traffic and by the time you reach the resort it is 5:15 p.m. It was only 24 miles and normal driving time for that distance is about a half hour! Remember to allow at least 1/3 more time for a bus transfer than the minutes you took when you drove that distance.

> **Allow at least 1/3 more time for a bus transfer than the time it takes to drive that distance.**

When possible, avoid heavy traffic in rush hours for bus transfers. In many cases this cannot be avoided so allow for extra time in your itinerary schedule. Most tour members are cooperative and understanding about extra lead time. When you explain the advantage to them they heartily agree because they dislike hurried pressure also. On occasions when it turns out that the lead time wasn't necessary, an early arrival just gives them a few unexpected personal minutes. They can use the extra time for the restroom, to browse a few minutes in a nearby gift shop, or to put a new roll of film in the camera.

Time Zone Differences

Often, a trip will take you and your group into a different time zone. This happens often with airline trips and with ground tours as well. Time differences will affect your tour planning in many ways.

The distance around the world is divided into one hour time zones. The international date line in the Pacific Ocean represents the beginning hour of each day. From that line the one hour time zones continue from east to west around the globe. Many large countries have several time zones within them. The distances between continents frequently totals six or seven zones — therefore, six or seven hour differences. Traveling in a westerly direction means that you will be subtracting hours from your departure time. Going in the opposite easterly direction you will be adding an hour for each time zone you pass through.

Your first group tours will probably take place within the United States and adjacent countries so you will need only to deal with the time zones that apply. As your trips extend to other continents, you will need to learn the time differences in various countries. Time zones within the United States and their abbreviations are as follows:

- East Coast:..... Eastern standard time, EST
- Midwest:........ Central standard time, CST
- West: .... Mountain standard time, MST
- West Coast: ... Pacific standard time, PST
- Hawaii: .... Hawaiian standard time, HST

Alaska is a very large state and has several zones.

Now, to further complicate your figuring on time periods, remember that daylight savings time is observed throughout the summer months in nearly all of the United States. This means that clocks are moved ahead one hour at the beginning of daylight time. Then they are moved back at the end of the summer period. Dates for these time adjustments are announced each year so that time listings become:

- East Coast:..... Eastern   daylight   time,   DST
  and so on.

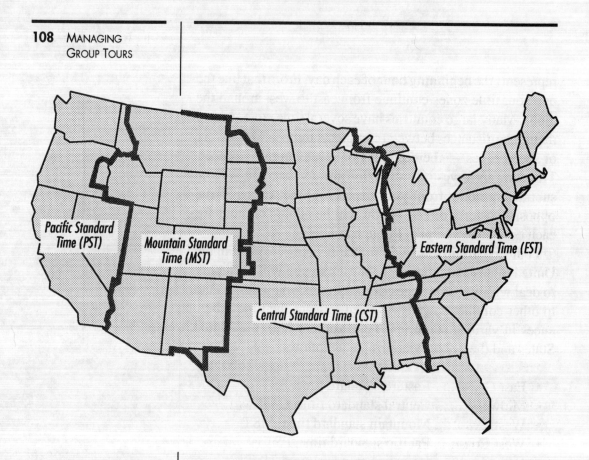

Pacific Standard Time (PST)

Mountain Standard Time (MST)

Eastern Standard Time (EST)

Central Standard Time (CST)

Unfortunately, the line which represents the time zone border does not always follow along state lines. Some states may be split into two different zones. To avoid confusion, that state may announce which of their time zones it will observe. In fact, a few states even choose not to move into daylight savings time and to remain on standard time throughout the entire year.

You are right to think that this may complicate your tour planning. You may often begin organizing a tour during one season, but it will actually occur in the following one. It is easy to neglect the time change possibilities when the shift seems a long while away. In order to avoid these problems, you will be wise to designate all of your hourly figures with the correct symbols. (eg., Arrive Dallas 4:15 p.m. CDT) By doing this, you are reminded to give conscious concern to the possible time differences.

When airline schedules are issued, the times are indicated in this manner, and you need to pay attention to those details. You also need to be able to explain and remind your tour participants about time zone differences. Many of them find it confusing and they need to understand how it will affect their trips.

Changing time zones will mean adding or subtracting hours to a day in the tour. Unfortunately, the human body doesn't adapt as quickly to the time change as the mind does. Therefore fatigue, hunger, and irregular sleep patterns can result. Always consider this when arranging tour activities and rest periods on your itinerary. After a day or so, your group will be much better able to cope with some of the more strenuous activities and enjoy them more. It is easiest to set up an itinerary with a structured form, such as the one shown on the next page. You may want to adapt it to your own needs as you work with it.

You should note in the example that each item that is being paid for the group (as a part of their tour price) is designated (included). You will also find that for each of these reserved activities the firm, telephone number and contact person is added. This information is necessary in case there is a need to clear up any confusion in the service being provided. There is usually no problem with a properly confirmed reservation, but at least you are prepared, just in case.

The memo column is to provide reminders for details that could be overlooked in busy times. After you have arrived in Denver and will be continuing in that time zone, you may not need to add the MTD to each hourly figure but be sure to resume that practice for your return flight.

When your itinerary is complete you should duplicate several copies — one for each person with responsibilities for the complete tour. The bus driver (on a motorcoach tour),

> **The human body doesn't adapt as quickly to the time change as the mind does.**

ITINERARY

TOUR: Colorado Holiday
GROUP: Business Women's Assn.

CONTACT: Marilyn Jones
(ph. 555-0934)

BEGINS: Thursday, June 22
ENDS: Monday, June 26
DESTINATION: Denver & surrounding area
TODAY: Thursday, June 22

TRANSPORTATION BY;
United Air Lines
Colorado Western Bus Line
Mountainview Tour Co.

Arrive	Depart	Itinerary Sequence	Memorandum
8:15 a.m. CDT		Passengers report to Metro Airport terminal in Case City, MN	Assemble at info desk, 2n level for check-in. Distribute tour packets.
	9:30 a.m. CDT	United Flight 105 departs - gate to be announced	
9:52 a.m. MDT		Arrive Stapleton Int'l Airport, Denver Reassemble at baggage claim area.	Time Change - set clocks back, 1 hour
	10:20 a.m. MDT	Board Colorado Western Bus 303/555-2500 (included) Conf. Loren	At east airport entrance, ground transportation area.
	10:30 a.m. MDT	Transfer to Holiday Inn, Downtown 1450 Glenarm Place 303/555-4322 Conf. Carolynn	
11:00 a.m. MDT		Deboard and check-in Brief welcome reception in the Garden Room	Baggage handled at this interval
12:30 p.m. MDT		Luncheon Buffet (included Conf. Florence	Dining room Holiday Inn
1:45 p.m. MDT		Group reassembles in lobby to depart for city tour	
	2:00 p.m. MDT	Board sightseeing bus at front entrance City tour (included) Mountainview Tour Co. 303-555-2927 Conf. Terry	Pay balance of fee to driver/guide
4:00 p.m. MDT		Return to Hotel Remainder of day on their own for convention activities.	

the escort, even the host (if you have one in a destination city) need to understand the sequence and timing you have planned. Most of all, you, as the tour director must have a copy with you at all times throughout the tour. Leave a master copy in your office file so persons at your "home base" can know exactly where and how to reach you in case of emergency.

There are many points in favor of independent operations in the tour business but there is one disadvantage that is always present. The success of the entire operation is dependent upon *you* to see it through. No matter how invincible we feel none of us is immune to emergencies, illness, accidents or a family crisis. These can prevent you from attending to details or perhaps from completing the trip. Good judgement demands that you designate a person who can serve as an alternate in such cases. You need to have your records complete so that your back-up person can step in and finish the tour. That person needs to know how to identify all of the people involved, how to proceed in your place, or how to cancel if necessary. Your forethought in planning with this person can protect you against many financial and legal problems and give you much needed peace of mind. Incidentally, use your back-up person's phone number for emergency contact throughout the tour.

> **The success of the entire operation is dependent upon you to see it through.**

Itineraries For Tour Participants

Just as you need an outline of the tour, so do the members of the tour group. They certainly don't need all of the details that you included in your own copy but they do need a general skeleton plan for each day throughout the tour. It will include scheduled times for meals, departures and arrivals, and special attractions and events planned for the day. It will tell them where the group will assemble, and which costs they will need to pay for themselves. A well-written member itinerary will help people look forward to each activity, know how to dress for an event, whether to take along a camera, and what kind of meals will be served. They can look forward to special activities, with enthusiasm and expectation. That is one of the important pleasures of any travel experience.

On the following page is an example of a day-to-day itinerary for tour members. You may want to duplicate and assemble these in the form of a purse or pocket-sized booklet, so they can be carried along throughout the trip.

TOURIST ITINERARY
Thursday, June 22

8:15 a.m. CDT   Arrive at Metro Airport terminal
Meet at Info. Desk for check-in

9:30 a.m. CDT   United Flight 105 departs
Gate to be announced

9:52 a.m. MDT   Arrive Denver Stapleton Airport
Meet group at baggage claim area

10:20 a.m. MDT   Board bus for transfer to hotel
(Included)

11:00 a.m. MDT   Arrive at Holiday Inn, Downtown
**Check in and welcome reception
(Included)**

12:30 p.m. MDT   Buffet lunch
Holiday dining room (Included)

1:45 p.m. MDT   Meet in lobby to depart for
City Tour (Included)

4:00 p.m. MDT   Return to hotel

Remainder of day, on your own, as convention opens the schedule of activities, at Convention Center — $1\frac{1}{2}$ blocks west of Holiday Inn. Opening session is dinner meeting in the ballroom at 6:30 p.m.

(The officers of the organization will provide further Convention details and announcements, so as tour director, you will not need to do so.)

Activity For Further Study

Plan a sample one-day tour for a group of people to go Christmas shopping in a large, well-known mall —in a city 75 miles from your town. They will travel by motorcoach, and will be home by 5:30 p.m.

Write up the itinerary as you would need to have it done for your planning.

Make-up a tour member's itinerary, too.

EFFECTIVE MARKETING

In every chapter we have referred to various marketing methods in the development of tour programs. This is not a coincidence. A sound marketing plan is the life-blood of any successful business venture. It is a framework for accomplishing your business goals.

Marketing is the process by which a product or service is sold to a buyer. In the tour business, we are dealing entirely with services. From the time a tour concept is originated, the continuing question is: will it be saleable to prospective buyers? The only way to answer that question is to determine what the buyers want and need. This is the beginning of market research for any service. A purchase requires the buyer to decide and then act on his decision. If he doesn't believe that he has a need for that service, he certainly is not going to be motivated to buy.

When we identify a customer's interests (which become needs) our challenge is to create a tour that will fit those needs. Then we have to locate all of the suppliers of the necessary services that will make such a tour possible. If we are fortunate, we find all of the right services and the tour can become a reality. Hopefully it will fill the expectations of the clients. A saleable package tour must have as many of those qualities as possible. This is the reason that careful planning is emphasized so much.

All of this process is further complicated by the fact that we will need a volume of clients to make that tour feasible. You may find a handful of people who are genuinely excited about your tour offering but a handful won't bring in profits. You need to search out other people, maybe not quite so motivated, or maybe simply unaware of the tour. You need to persuade them that this tour will fill a need for them, too. This is where promotion becomes important. We can accomplish this by:

- making certain that every possible customer knows that this tour is available (advertising)
- convincing clients that the rewards of this tour will fill their needs and desires (eg., a chance to relax on a getaway weekend or escape from the winter doldrums to sunny Florida)
- including other attractive features that will enhance the tour experience (eg., free golf and tennis privileges at the resort or some special entertainment events included
- eliminating every possible apprehension which may limit their interest (eg., assure them of quality accommodations and emphasize the excellent price for all that is included)

Consumer Confidence

One of the most powerful forces in selling is the development of a client's confidence. People tend to avoid dealing with individuals and companies that they don't know. As we mentioned before, this calls for an early effort for you and your company to become as visible as possible in your city or area. If you are already well acquainted with many people, you have an advantage. Participating in organizations and public events will help you to make even more contacts. People will feel more comfortable if they have seen your company's services listed in the yellow pages of the local telephone directory. For a relatively low fee, you can reserve a space to announce your company name, address, phone, office hours, and a brief list of your types of tours.

Your local newspaper probably has a travel page that could supply you with advertising space periodically. This is a good way to promote general (assembled) tours and hopefully gain new travelers. If the paper has a fairly large circulation (30 to 50,000 or more) your ad may reach a good number of readers. Such advertisements may be costly depending upon the size of the space you use. Regular advertisers are usually given better rates but until your tours are fairly frequent that may not be a help to you. Your newspaper advertisement can be used to publicize a series of tours or an individual trip. In either case, it must be well designed to be effective.

Newspaper Advertising

- Choose a headline that is clear and impressive.
- Use a border to make the ad standout from others on the page.
- Plan the art work and printing to be simple, uncrowded, and easy to read.
- Give accurate information in a simple language that readers can understand.
- Include pertinent data: destination, date(s), price, and basic features of the trip.
- Be sure to include your company name and phone number for reservation purposes.

You probably won't need newspaper advertisements for your affiliated group trips (organizations and agencies). Marketing for them is usually done within their own groups.

Magazines

You see advertisements by large tour firms and cruise companies in magazines every day. Many are impressive full page artistic creations with appealing messages. These are also very costly of course, but they are effective in drawing massive reservations and establishing the operator's image. Smaller tours simply cannot justify such expensive promotions. But you can study the style and approach they use. You'll find some excellent ideas for your own publicity efforts.

Radio & Television

One of the most expensive ways to advertise is by broadcasting. Not only is there a cost for preparing the film clip or presentation but your company also has to buy air time from the radio/television station. Repeated showings may reach a larger number of viewers but will increase the cost.

There is one possible way that you might be able to obtain some broadcast exposure. Local talk show hosts sometimes invite organization representatives for a personal interview about their projects or special events. If you are promoting a custom tour for such an organization, they might be able to announce their tour plans as part of a guest appearance program. It would probably be a one-exposure session, but at least it is personal and direct.

Brochures & Flyers

One of the best ways to circulate news about tour offerings is by distributing brochures and flyers. These are relatively inexpensive and can be used in a variety of ways.

Brochures are often used to announce a listing of tours for the season. They provide the destinations, dates, prices and a brief description of each tour. This is a good device for long range planning. It offers a number of choices that you could present during a discussion with a group chairman. Although the listing will probably include only the assembled tours, you could also add the trips for special groups, too. That may generate enough interest that you could offer a similar tour for general public travelers.

Your first attempts at creating brochures don't have to be complicated. You can make it attractive and interesting by using clip art and details about tour features. You might even want to encourage "early bird" reservations with a small discount. If you create your own brochures, they can be duplicated in quantity at a copy service shop.

A flyer is usually designed to advertise a single tour and generally limited to one page. This device is an ideal way to put complete information about a trip into the customers' hands. It can be as artistic and detailed as you wish, but it must:

- have an attention-getting headline
- state the destination and activities as planned
- list the date(s) and times of departure and return
- state the price, deposit and payment schedule
- include reservation procedures
- name the tour firm and source for more information
- include a disclaimer statement (the limit of the tour operator's responsibility and liability)

Attractive flyers can be inexpensively designed with clip art and a supply of press-on letters. Fill in the rest with your typewriter and you can paste up a good flyer very easily. If you are skilled at graphic arts, you may be able to create clever illustrations of your own. If you work with a computer, you already know how versatile it is in creating clever and original copy. You might want to duplicate your copies on colored paper for additional interest.

On the following pages are examples of a promotional flyer and a seasonal brochure.

One of the best ways to circulate news about tour offerings is by distributing brochures and flyers.

**Postage rates
continue to soar so
try to find other
ways to distribute
flyers.**

You will receive a more accurate response with a clip-out reservation form. Be sure to include the disclaimer statement, as shown in the illustration. You can type it and reduce it to small print but be sure to use it for your own protection. In the very unlikely event that a supplier provides faulty service, you will be protected against liability. It rarely happens, but it only takes one time, and an exploitive client to produce legal problems for you.

Try to find ways to distribute flyers so they don't have to be mailed. Postage rates continue to be a major cost and can reduce your profits. One good time to pass out flyers for a future trip, is during the return segment of a tour. The passengers are enjoying the exhilaration of their trip and mentally concluding that tours are a good "way to go." Distribute them early enough on the return segment that good friends can discuss them and plan together. Some will even leave their reservations and checks with you as they depart.

You may also want to provide a supply of flyers to your Chamber of Commerce or Visitor's Bureau. It has even proved helpful to post copies of flyers and brochures on bulletin boards in retirement centers or in bus stations and airline terminals. You should check to see if such a posting is restricted in those areas, however.

Newsletters

After your tour program is well under way, you might want to set up a newsletter distribution. A monthly or seasonal issue will give you the chance to send out information on upcoming tour offerings. Space for a personal greetings can express your delight in tours just completed. You might also include some pictures of a recent tour group. Choose a clever name for your publication and include one or two general interest items such as:

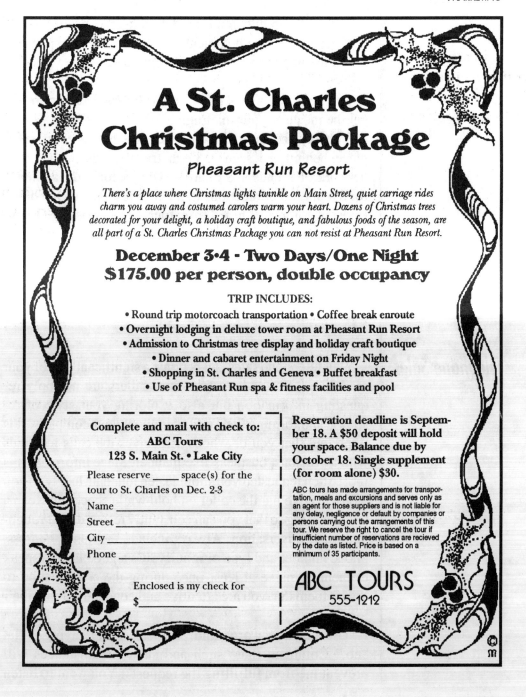

A St. Charles Christmas Package

Pheasant Run Resort

There's a place where Christmas lights twinkle on Main Street, quiet carriage rides charm you away and costumed carolers warm your heart. Dozens of Christmas trees decorated for your delight, a holiday craft boutique, and fabulous foods of the season, are all part of a St. Charles Christmas Package you can not resist at Pheasant Run Resort.

December 3·4 - Two Days/One Night
$175.00 per person, double occupancy

TRIP INCLUDES:

- Round trip motorcoach transportation • Coffee break enroute
- Overnight lodging in deluxe tower room at Pheasant Run Resort
- Admission to Christmas tree display and holiday craft boutique
- Dinner and cabaret entertainment on Friday Night
- Shopping in St. Charles and Geneva • Buffet breakfast
- Use of Pheasant Run spa & fitness facilities and pool

Complete and mail with check to:
ABC Tours
123 S. Main St. • Lake City

Please reserve _____ space(s) for the tour to St. Charles on Dec. 2-3

Name _____

Street _____

City _____

Phone _____

Enclosed is my check for

$ _____

Reservation deadline is September 18. A $50 deposit will hold your space. Balance due by October 18. Single supplement (for room alone) $30.

ABC tours has made arrangements for transportation, meals and excursions and serves only as an agent for those suppliers and is not liable for any delay, negligence or default by companies or persons carrying out the arrangements of this tour. We reserve the right to cancel the tour if insufficient number of reservations are recieved by the date as listed. Price is based on a minimum of 35 participants.

ABC TOURS
555-1212

- the new grandparent/grandchild tours concept
- dates when the botanical gardens are at their splendor
- a list of summer festivals in your area

You can always tuck in a flyer or two for future tours and get the most for your mailing.

Probably the most effective advertising for tours takes place behind the scenes. Each traveler has his/her own network of friends and relatives who become the audience for a report on or reactions to the tour just taken. One of the frequent comments heard from tour members is "Wait until I tell my family (or neighbor) about this!" It is an important part of the trip experience to share it in descriptive conversation. An enthusiastic report is guaranteed to produce phone calls to your business with requests to be added to the mailing list or reserved for the next tour.

Telephone Sales

Your telephone sales can become a significant part of your marketing effort. Many first-time callers are not only requesting information but also exploring your style of response and forming their attitudes about your company. It is important that you or whoever receives the calls responds with a gracious, business-like manner. Since information is most often requested you should keep tour data handy so you won't need to put the caller on hold while checking. Keep a telephone log so that you can constantly record data throughout your conversation. Always include the name, address, phone number and type of inquiry. It's a good idea to speak to them by name at least once during the conversation to assure them that you are attentive and concerned about their inquiry.

Use positive words and phrases. Avoid saying a flat "no." Comment that "such and such circumstances will prevent me from fulfilling the request". You want to listen

**Keep a telephone
log so that you can
constantly record
data throughout
your conversation.**

attentively to the personal information as the caller some-times rambles on, but try to find effective ways to return to the business of the call without being abrupt. Learn to confirm a conversation with a summary statement such as "I'm glad you called about…" and confirm your response action. For example, "…and I'll have your name on the reservation list just as soon as I receive your check. I'll be watching for it in the mail." Now you are both clear about it.

Incidentally, your telephone voice and speech are equally important sales tools. A thin, timid, higher pitched voice does not generate rapport and trust as well as a lower, mellow confident approach. You may want to listen to a tape record-ing of some of your conversations to evaluate how well you are conveying your professionalism and enthusiasm. With a little practice, you can change your voice level and style for good results.

If you cannot be certain that your phone inquiries are regularly covered, you may want to install an answer-ing machine. If you do, you should plan your outgoing message with care. Be sure to identify yourself and your company by name. In a clear and gracious state-ment, invite the caller to leave a message. Always remind them to include their phone number so you can return their call. Be sure to respond promptly to all telephone messages left on the machine. You may want to purchase multiple call recording tapes so you can keep used ones at least a few months for reference purposes. Sometimes it is very helpful to be able to check a back tape to document some bit of information at the source.

Your telephone charges are a significant part of your business expenses. You might be wise to install a separate line for your business purposes otherwise charges may easily become confused with your personal calls. As your business volume grows, you will probably want to arrange

Longer Trips – More Fun!

May 9-12
4 days - 3 nights - 6 meals

$350
double occupancy

National Convention In Detroit
American Association of Retired Persons
It is a great convention! Hear outstanding speakers such as David Horowitz, Dr. Art Ulene, Jane Bryant Quinn, Raplh Nader and Louis Rukeyser. A special "Evening of Jazz" concert, too. All planned for you - meals, lodging at the Dearborn Holiday Inn and sightseeing. Also included is a visit to the Holland Tulip Festival, admission to Henry Ford Museum and Greenfield Village and a city tour.

On The Shores of Lake Michigan...
A three day summer holiday at a resort on the shores of Lake Michigan. Stroll the beach, swim, sit in the sun and just relax. The lake shore area is beautiful and so peaceful. We'll take an outing to Milwaukee one day. On the way home we'll stop at the Chicago Botanical Gardens.

June 14-16
3 days - 2 nights - 3 meals

$245
double occupancy

July 16-17
2 days - 1 nights - 2 meals

$210
double occupancy

Weekend in St. Louis...
There is so much to see and do in St. Louis - and this is your chance for a mini-holiday in the city. There will be a tour of the city, time at Forest Park and the Botanical Gardens and a great evening on the Goldenrod Showboat with their dinner and show. The trip includes lodging at the Holiday Inn, excursions and of course, the special enternment.

Music City, USA - Nashville!
Nashville, Tennessee welcomes you to a wonderful weekend holiday. You'll have reserved seats at the Grand Old Opry and a full day in Opryland Park. Top it all off with a dinner cruise and show on the General Jackson Showboat. Included - two nights lodging, three meals and of course, transportation.

September 3-5
3 days - 2 nights - 3 meals

$380
double occupancy

ABC TOURS

1221 S. MAIN ST.   LAKE CITY, WA 5400   555-1212

Sales Management

for an 800 number but it is not necessary in the early stages of your tour business.

Handling customer sales is a continuing job from the time you announce the tour to the day you reach reservation deadlines. Customers can pay for their trips in two ways. They can turn in their checks or cash to the travel chairman of the organization or residence center. That person will then forward the funds to you along with a complete list of tour members, their addresses and their telephone numbers. Be sure the list indicates whether it was paid by check or cash.

In many cases, however, customers may send their checks directly to you. If you are affiliated with an agency, you should specify that checks should be mailed to your personal address rather than the agency address. Be sure that you have a full name for each customer. The address is usually available from the check. Occasionally, you will receive a request from a customer who would like to pay by credit card. This is more frequently the case with multi-day tours when travelers would like to use the benefit of the automatic travel insurance available from some credit card companies. Generally, it is not wise to accept credit card payments. For one reason, the handling of a possible refund is time consuming and complex. In addition, you have even more ledger book work and you surely do not want that at this time.

> As with all business transactions, the customer needs to have some kind of verification of his/her reservation and payment.

As with all business transactions, the customer needs to have some kind of verification of his/her reservation and payment. It they are paying in person, most tour companies simply hand them a receipt.

For a mailed reservation it is important to send the customer a receipt and confirmation letter. If they have paid a deposit with the balance due later, it helps to acknowledge the reservation and remind them about the date of the balance due. You may want to develop a confirmation form that you can fill out quickly and mail with the receipt. Here is an example that could be used for your form.

Glad You're Going Along!

Thank you for your check and reservation for the trip to _____

on (dates) _____

Deposit _____

Balance _____ Due on _____

Sharing room with _____

Departure date _____ Time _____

Location _____

I'll be sending you a letter soon with details about our trip. In the meantime, please call me if you have any questions or concerns. Ph. 555-2345

Sincerely,
Marilyn Jones, Director
ABC Tours

When a customer cancels the trip, you need to acknowledge it immediately. Be sure to record that same change in plans on your customer lists. Again, you may want to develop a simple form that you could send along with the refund check.

Dear

I'm sorry that you need to cancel your plans for your trip to:_____

on (dates)_____

Enclosed is a check in the amount of _____ for your refund. See you on the next tour!

Sincerely,
Marilyn Jones, Director
ABC Tours

Cancellations

You need to refer now to the policies you set up when you started your business. Usually, a cancellation turned in by the deadline date will be honored by a full refund. If that date has passed you need to determine the percentage of refund that will be withheld as a penalty. Usually, a 25% cancellation fee is appropriate but you may need to adjust that amount relative to your computations. Most suppliers allow some variations in your final numbers. Maybe there will be one or two over or under the original estimate. Some of your reservations are paid in advance and are non-refundable. Or perhaps when you reserve a motorcoach, a firm price is quoted regardless of the number of passengers. You tried to prorate that amount into the price of each person's cost, but cancellations mean empty seats and a balance of the charge that will come from your profits.

A cancellation penalty tends to discourage impulsive travelers from a quick change of mind. It also helps you, as the operator, cover most of the non-refundable charges that you may be forced to pay because of the cancellation.

Now, suppose that due to such a low number of reservations received, you decide that it would not be wise to complete the tour. This time, *you* are the person to cancel. If you will remember, you reserved the right to do so in your disclaimer statement. However, you must do so before the deadline dates of any of your suppliers. If you don't, you too will be paying penalties or losing deposits. Determine the date and stick to it.

When you do decide to cancel, it is important to notify your reserved travelers immediately by phone with apologies, a reason why, and the promise of a full refund promptly. Again, mail out the cancellation form along with their refund checks. At the same time, contact every supplier and verify in writing that your plans with them are cancelled. Then specify what your payments to them have been for refundable deposits and request the refunds. Keep copies of those letters in your tour folder for reference purposes.

All of this correspondence might seem unnecessary when you could just as easily telephone your contact person at each of the suppliers. But it isn't always possible to reach that person immediately and his/her secretary's memo to be passed along may not reach the contact person by the deadline date. Just be certain and put it all in writing.

Cancellations mean empty seats and a balance of the charge that will come from your profits.

**Be certain and
put everything
in writing.**

With each cancelled trip, you need to do a serious re-evaluation of that tour. Try to discover why it didn't draw the response you had expected and how you can avoid that result in the future. It is no disaster to cancel a trip now and then, but a customer may soon begin to be wary after his reservations are dropped several times. It may be a problem to regain the client's interest and by word of mouth his disappointment spreads to his friends and associates.

Do the best you can to promote your tours throughout your booking period. You should also be aware that many people wait until near the deadline date to reserve. They may be uncertain about their personal plans, health or whether they will have the money. It is always interesting that many senior citizens wait to reserve until they have received their social security or benefit checks at the beginning of a month. They may not have the need to do so for available funds, but somehow, the assurance that financial resources are still there gives them the encouragement to spend. In fact, older folks are often loathe to plan many things very far ahead. Perhaps experience has taught them that the future is uncertain, even for the best laid plans. As one sweet older lady explained once, "We just don't count too much on time ahead — we don't even buy green bananas."

Take these factors into consideration when you are anxious about sign-ups. Well-planned and strongly promoted trips to fascinating and appealing places will invariably draw people to your tours.

*Activity For
Further Study*

1. Write a tour description for a tour, similar to those in the brochure. Be sure that it is descriptive and informative, yet appealing.

2. Design a tour flyer that could be used to promote a group tour. Be sure to include the disclaimer statement.

ESCORTING THE TOUR

The reservation deadline has arrived and your tour has filled. Maybe there are even a few extra customers that you could place on a waiting list. Don't hesitate to do so. A last-minute cancellation may make it possible for one or more to go, even at a late date. However, do not overfill a tour beyond capacity anticipating cancellations and no shows. That is exactly when they don't happen and you are in an embarrassing spot with disgruntled tour members.

Pre-tour Preparations

You can now contact your suppliers with exact numbers of tour members and the balance of payments if required. For multi-day trips, the hotels send a form for a rooming list so you can clarify which members are sharing double rooms and if anybody requested single rooms. Return it to them promptly and keep a copy for your own files.

The tour members are looking forward to the trip. By this time you have either scheduled a pre-trip meeting or sent a letter with details and helpful instructions. They should have the receipt for balance of payment, name tags, luggage tags and their own itinerary sheet of tour events. In your pre-tour letter, be sure to include your telephone number so they can call you if they have questions. Most of them won't, but they enjoy the feeling of security in knowing that they can do so.

Perspectives

As you look forward to the trip you need to clarify exactly what you hope will happen. You hope that:

- The sequence of each segment of the tour will occur smoothly.
- The tour members will feel a belongingness in the group and demonstrate cooperative attitudes.
- The attractions of the tour are equal to or beyond the members' expectations.
- As customers, members will return from the trip satisfied from time and money well-spent, anticipating the next tour.

As they arrive for boarding you may be impressed at the wide variety of individuals who have assembled for this tour. With so many different personality types, you wonder whether they will develop bonds for group feelings. It is a short jaunt (a one- or two-day excursion) so they may not and it probably won't make a lot of difference whether they do. But an extended trip will function better all around if group bonding develops.

Benefits Of A Strong Group

We have already recognized that tourists enjoy their trips more when they share them with congenial companions. Besides that, the role of a tour leader is much easier with a strong supportive group. Gradually, they begin to "look out" for each other:

- reminding one another about procedures and plans
- assisting with minor difficulties (a broken luggage strap or a misplaced raincoat)
- avoiding confusion, crowding and urgency

It's fascinating to observe certain individuals take on special roles and begin to serve the others needs. You'll hear, "Ask Harry about adjusting your camera. He seems to know a lot about them". Or, "I'll meet you back here for lunch. But be on time, I don't want to be late".

An effective group can actually help keep one another in line by their consistent behavior and language. A non-conforming person soon begins to realize that he/she wouldn't be tolerated with actions in poor taste or abusive style.

The Group Leaders Role

To be an effective tour director, you need to function within a careful balance of business efficiency and personal consideration. The group needs to know you as a gracious, pleasant, and confident leader who takes your responsibilities seriously. You need to show them that you know what you are doing and that you function well. Yet, as a friendly, caring person, you never really become a part of the group but always maintain your authority role. You have to do this in order to carry out the tour plan. It also lets them know that they have a person in charge to keep things going right and safely. You become a sort of "velvet hammer" in the system.

Passengers As Individuals

Whether your group assembles at a pre-tour meeting or at boarding time, you should greet each person in a warm, friendly manner. Introduce yourself and get their names in mind. As you check them off on the passenger list, be sure you know the right pronunciation, and note if one mentions... "I'm Robert Jones, Call me Bob." No matter how much you have on your mind, give your full attention to a person's inquiry or request. Handle it quickly, but not abruptly, and with a response that deals with the concern.

Be sure that each person has a name tag. It helps you to learn names and for people to become acquainted with each other. It also helps when the group is being admitted at an event and even in emergencies. See Appendix #14 for suggestions about design and use of name tags.

Communication With Groups

As a source of information, you will often be speaking to the tour group. What you say and how you speak makes a great deal of difference in your relationship with the group.

Always wait until the whole group is present before you make your announcements. Speak clearly and slowly enough that they can understand you. Use a public address system if one is available. Even if you need to speak loudly, it should not be a shouting effort. Keep your tone of voice pleasant and stable.

Use language that is appropriate to the age group and without slang or rough phrases. Use positive statements. (Rather than "don't" say "to avoid _____, be sure to _____"). Look directly at the group, making eye contact among the people.

Make your general comments first and save the precise directions for your latter statements. Folks will remember them better and follow through. Always give an opportunity for questions from the group. Repeat the question for the group to hear and give the answer. As you close the session, repeat the immediate instruction in a condensed form for those who may have missed it. Try to avoid extended periods of directions and discussions. After four or five minutes, some folks will begin to tune you out. It would be better to save the extra instructions for a time nearer to the situation when they will be needed.

Encouraging Group Response

There are several ways that you can develop your group's responsiveness. Try some of these:

- "Give yourselves a hand for all getting here right on time!" *(Applause)*
- "Did all of you enjoy that show as much as I did?" *(Applause)*

Recognize a tour member for a special reason -

- "Fred and Aletha Jones are celebrating their 33rd wedding anniversary today. Congratulations!" *(Applause and comments)*

Appreciation for a significant effort—

- "We all want to thank Bill (bus driver) for a comfortable, safe trip, and all of those stops so we could take pictures." *(Applause)*

This is their way of communicating in unison. And, did you notice, each response was for a tour supporting comment! The subtle message that they are expressing is approval for the tour and for each other.

Seat Rotations

Because all seats on a motorcoach are not equal, tour members need to have a smooth and convenient rotation system. This is especially true when you are traveling through scenic areas or when long periods of time are spent on the coach. If they have intervals on other kinds of transportation then it is not quite so critical to rotate seating. Generally it is wise to set up the system and adhere to it to avoid controversy.

You should begin the trip with assigned seats. From your

chart, as the passengers board the bus, you can assign their seats by row number and indicate whether it is on the drivers side or the door side. Be sure to seat friends or companions in adjacent seats for their pleasure. After your trip is on its way, you can explain your rotation system. Make it as simple as possible by using your microphone so all of them can hear. Preface your remarks with: "So that every person will have an equal chance to share in the preferred seats, let's follow this plan. When we return to the bus tomorrow morning (or after lunch), or what ever the interval of time may be, remember to move one seat forward. The front row passengers will move to the back row on the same side of the coach."

You can remind them to move their travel items (raincoat, shopping bag, etc.) to the seat ahead as they leave the bus. Then it will remind them of their new seat location.

It's a good idea to rotate seats at a stop-over and usually after half-day periods have passed. Always remind them at the end of a day so they will be in the proper seat the next morning.

There are exceptions in seating patterns, of course. The public address microphone is usually located at the seat just behind the driver. This should be reserved for the tour leader or escort. Occasionally, a tour member who is handicapped will need to be seated near the exit for ease in boarding and deboarding. Keep this in mind when you are assigning the other seats which can be rotated.

> It's a good idea
> to rotate seats
> at a stop-over
> and usually after
> half-day periods
> have passed.

Group Procedures

One of the ways that you can build the group's confidence is through your handling of routine matters. They need to move so smoothly that errors are nearly impossible. For example, there are dozens of times when the group assembles and reassembles for transfers at various locations. Always be sure to state clearly the time and place you plan for them to meet. It even helps to point out a landmark that they can identify so they can be sure.

The most important factor is that you should be there, early enough and visible, so that first arrivals will know they are in the right place. If you are meeting a motorcoach, remind the driver to be there in plenty of time too. Again, you are just preventing anxious moments.

When you arrive at an event or restaurant, a similar kind of prethinking will help you. Avoid the tiring period of standing in line in a crowded lobby. Ask the group to remain on the bus while you go inside to check if they are ready for your group. Then, all you need to do is signal the group and they enter without delay.

Leave an event a little before the end of the performance so you can be sure that the bus is in place and ready for departure. Check members off with your passenger list as they reboard and you'll be sure everyone is there without "counting noses" again and again.

Hotels, Motels & Resorts

The managements of lodging accommodations have developed excellent ways to simplify the check-in and checkout procedures for tour groups. By requesting the rooming lists from you in advance, all of the time- consuming check-in was pre-arranged by the hotel staff. When your group arrives at the hotel, you alone report to the registration desk to pick up the waiting packets of room keys. When you return to the bus or van to distribute the packets, each tour member can go directly to his assigned room.

Arrangements for baggage handling are equally smooth. When you sent in the rooming list, a number was assigned to each passenger. You marked each luggage tag with the proper number. As the group arrives, the porters automatically pick up the numbered pieces of luggage and take them to the assigned rooms.

**Many hotels
plan a brief
welcome reception
for the group.**

Many hotels plan a brief welcome reception for the group (with punch and cookies) to occupy the tour members for a few minutes while the baggage is being distributed. It's a nice gesture and it does prevent confusion.

Since lodging accommodations are usually included in the tour price, you will handle the check-out and final payment procedures. Well before your actual departure, the porters will pick up luggage from the rooms and deliver it to the waiting motorcoach. All that your tour members need to do is pay any personal charges they may have incurred. The group is then on its way again.

Some resorts and cruise lines even provide baggage transfer back to the airport, where it can be automatically checked in for the flight home. There is an additional charge for these services, but many groups are willing to pay for it.

Enroute

As you were planning the itinerary for your tour, you were able to arrange the periods of activity and rest to allow for variety and interest. However, nearly every trip involves some continued hours of transportation and limited opportunity to plan pastimes. Fortunately, most people are resourceful enough to bring along some reading materials. Conversations with a seat partner will help to fill some time too.

Most domestic flights are only a couple hours at the most. Even if there are two or more segments of air travel, there is at least a stopover in the airport for a bit of diversion. As a tour director, you will need to provide tour packets and instructions before the flight departure. You will be with the group for the trip, but the flight attendants usually handle the routine concerns efficiently.

On the other hand, train or bus travel may require considerably more consecutive hours. Remember to schedule a motorcoach rest stop every couple of hours. These welcome breaks can be planned at a highway rest area, a scenic place, or at a quickie fast food restaurant. In any case, there should be adequate facilities available. Your group will need easily accessible restrooms that are clean and with several stalls. There should also be fresh, safe drinking water and space for people to move about and stretch their muscles a bit.

All coaches now restrict smoking on board so these stops are a pleasant relief for desperate smokers. You may want to include a few sticks of gum or some mints in the passengers' on-board packets to help smokers during their prolonged travel hours.

If the hours between meals are long, your travelers may relish some refreshment at the break. Your stop at a restaurant would give them a chance to get a quick snack or a soft drink. Remember though, this will take more time, especially for sit-down service. Carry outs are quicker, but people will be eating on the bus. Be prepared with trash bags so you can quickly clear any smelly leftover debris.

You might want to provide a quick refreshment of your own at a rest area or scenic spot. Plan ahead with a quantity thermos of coffee, disposable cups, and packets of sweetener and creamer. If you use decaffeinated coffee, everyone can drink it and there is no consternation about some person's inability to handle regular coffee.

With a little more effort you could supply doughnuts or cookies. But remember, all of these little extras add up as hidden costs so include them in your tour budget.

> **Nearly every trip involves some continued hours of transportation.**

On-Board Food

Sometimes a meal on board is necessary to save time and money, but it involves some careful selection to obtain appropriate foods and beverages. You should choose items such as sandwiches that can be eaten with no utensils. In most cases, you have no facilities to keep foods warm or to reheat them so you will depend on foods that can be safely transported and kept chilled. Various types of sandwiches, relishes, fresh fruit, cup cakes and cookies are the usual standby choices. But with a little creative planning, even these box lunches can be nourishing and appetizing. A word of warning however: all foods must be sanitary and safe from possible spoilage. The possible results are not worth the gamble.

On-board beverages should be served in no-spill containers, preferably with handled cups or mugs. Cold drinks are a little simpler to serve and transport. Watch for serving size containers (cans or cartons) that can be opened as needed. Purchased by the case, they are more economical. Again, you are dealing with cost factors that must be added into your pricing plan.

On-Board Activities

Learn to sense the intervals when tedium and boredom can develop within a group. You can recognize these when conversation has faded to a minimum as many people stare expressionless out the window and several have fallen asleep. Don't be alarmed at an occasional lull like this. Everyone needs a chance to relax and retreat into his own private thoughts once in a while. Sometimes the group experience can become tiresome and a nap will refresh and renew the traveler.

One way to prevent periods of boredom is by planning for it in advance. Include a few items in the tour packets for pastime activities. You might use an intriguing crossword puzzle, a brain teaser, or some fascinating information leaflets to read. (Be sure that they are in fairly large print, easy to read, and on general interest topics.) On longer trips you may want to bring along a small carton of activity items such as playing cards, Rubiks cubes (or similar games), and an assortment of current magazines. Some deluxe trains and buses are equipped with fold-up tables that can be used for group games and activities. These are great ways to shorten the time on a long journey.

On longer trips, bring along activity items such as playing cards and magazines.

Sometimes you may want to provide some group entertainment to dispel the boredom. Again, the possibilities will depend upon the resources you have at hand. On a bus that is equipped with a stereo music system, you could supply a tape of pleasant relaxing music to be played. (Not too loud because some of the speakers are too close for comfort, and not for a long time either because spontaneous conversation is always more important than background music.)

If your motorcoach has a closed circuit television system, you could play a movie cassette that the passengers would enjoy. Choose an up-to-date film with a fairly simple plot and an upbeat and amusing sequence. Avoid involved, mood producing films no matter how great the critics may have rated them to be. Be sure to know how to turn off the speaker or set at the locations of disinterested persons who prefer to read or sleep. Also, be ready to interrupt the movie for an interval when you happen to come upon a spectacular sight or special interest. Remember that they can see a movie any time and the aspects of the tour have first priority.

As you arrive at or pass through a particular area, it is helpful for you to provide a brief summary about things the group is seeing. If you search out the data a bit before the tour, you can attach that paragraph to your itinerary folder and be ready to read it (or tell it) at the appropriate time. For example, as you come to the Great Salt Lake area in Utah and see the miles of salt flats, you could explain to them:

The miles of salt flats we see here are the result of a million year history of the Great Salt Lake. The Great Salt Lake is the largest body of salt water in the Northern Hemisphere and one of the most salty bodies of water in the world. It was formed more than two million years ago by the shifting of the earth's surface—and finally filled by the flow of water from the glacier ice. It was originally a huge lake, named Lake Bonneville. At that time it was 300 miles long

It is helpful for you to provide a brief summary about things the group is seeing.

and over 900 feet deep. It has gradually shrunk from evaporation into three separate lakes—Great Salt Lake, Lake Provo, and Lake Sevier. The Great Salt Lake was discovered and named in 1824 by James Bridger, who explored the area and established trading posts.

Today the Great Salt Lake is fed by the Bear, Weber, and Jordan Rivers and it has no outlet. It varies greatly in size, depending upon evaporation and the flow of rivers that feed it. It is about 1600 square miles in size now, and its average depth is generally less than 15 feet. The salt flats are ideal for automobile and motorcycle speed trails and races. You probably have heard of the Bonneville Flats competitions and the speed records that have been set there.

All of this advance preparation may seem to be a great deal of effort, but there are many benefits to be gained. Your enthusiasm for new information is contagious and sets a key for the learning opportunities that travel offers. It enhances the whole experience and increases the value of the tour.

There are many benefits to be gained by being prepared.

Lagniappe is the term Texans use for these thoughtful efforts. It's an extra complimentary gesture given as good will to a purchaser. It certainly isn't necessary, and it can always be offered when your time and energy allow. Most travelers are impressed and appreciative for your efforts.

There are many other kinds of group activities possible and you can use your best judgement in selecting appropriate ones. You may choose some of the ideas offered in the Appendix. In general, it is better to use a brief, fun activity that is fairly non-intellectual at first. Sometimes even telling a humorous experience or a clever joke may be a good approach. Whatever you choose, it should be in good taste and free from rough language, poor grammar, suggestive remarks and prejudicial comments. Not only would you appear unprofessional, it may also violate your tour members' feelings.

Guard against the temptation to spend too much time on the speaker system with frequent interruptions. Plan ahead what they need to know and present it without rambling on. It is a good idea to avoid personal information in your discussions although they may be curious and interested. A professional leader is always aware of the danger of revealing much of his/her personal life and feelings. It seems to destroy the sense of status of a leader and can make him/her vulnerable to evaluative remarks and comments. Keep your focus on the tour and the people who are involved.

By maintaining a level of reserve, you will be more able to retain your role as leader at all times. Your group needs to be aware that you are making this whole tour happen because you are in control. They all want the tour to proceed and without your leadership the necessary policies cannot be enforced. You enjoy the informal fun the group is sharing, but always with a poise and dignity that will protect your authority. This is a delicate but important balance to maintain. It silently states that you won't let things go too far or get out of hand.

Your demeanor is the gauge by which your group knows its limits. A highly inappropriate remark needs only for you to look directly at the person with a calm, serious comment such as "We don't need that." Then quickly look away and engage in other conversation. If two or more people are producing the annoyance, again a direct look at them with a serious "We want no more of that." Then turn to your microphone and start discussing some aspect of the upcoming itinerary, subtly restating your status and authority.

Very rarely, an individual becomes so irritating and abusive that his/her behavior is spoiling the tour events for the group. A private discussion with the person and his/her travel companion will often change the behavior. However, if it

Problem Situations

Your demeanor is the gauge by which your group knows its limits.

**Good commun-
ication is the key
to all positive
relationships.**

seems futile to try to tolerate the situation, it is best to ask the person to leave the tour group and assist them in arranging their personal transportation home. Later, explain the problem objectively and professionally to your tour members and drop the issue. They will be as glad as you are to put it all behind and move ahead with pleasurable activities.

You can avoid many complications by informing, even warning, your travelers about customs and legal regulations that could be carelessly violated. If such a situation does arise, your tourist bureau contacts can advise you about getting necessary assistance. Again, the most valuable resource you have is a strong group that helps to monitor developing problems. Good communication is the key to all positive relationships.

Activities For Further Study

1. Make a list of the materials and supplies a tour director or escort should take along on each tour.

2. Write a brief summary of information about some site that you know well. Be sure to include interesting fact that will appeal to the tour members.

EMERGENCIES

CHAPTER TWELVE

In spite of all of the pre-planning and good intentions, there are occasional crises that involve the members of tour groups. By considering the best ways to handle such moments in advance, we are generally more prepared and there are fewer negative consequences. Let's look at some of them.

Delays, Breakdowns and Weather

Some of the interruptions relate to the carrier: the train, bus or plane. If the problem is a simple delay such as a cancelled flight, equipment breakdown, or weather problem, it usually is a matter of rescheduling and change in itinerary. As soon as information is definite about the circumstances, you need to let your tour members know. It is best done by gathering everyone together as a group in an area where they can all hear the same facts and instructions. Don't tell a few and ask them to pass the word along. You'd be amazed at the distorted information that reached the last listeners.

In your announcement, simply state facts and express the disappointment that "we all share." Then assure them that efforts to correct the situation will be prompt. Depending upon the location, devise a preoccupation for the interval of the delay such as an early lunch or time to shop at a nearby area. Specify a time for their return to your location. Above all, you need to be there when they do return so you can proceed from there.

Call your next suppliers (restaurant, attraction or entertainment) as soon as possible to alert them about your delay. Find out whether they can provide their service later. When your situation is corrected, be sure to contact them again with definite adaptation to your plans.

If you are stranded in a forsaken spot, it may be better for the group to remain on the bus. Try to innovate some activity during the waiting time and do not appear agitated or unduly worried. If you are lucky, the bus driver will join in with some interesting or amusing anecdotes and the time could be thoroughly enjoyable.

It is most important to remain calm and reassuring.

Accidents

In case of an accident, the first concern is deboarding passengers, summoning help, and keeping everyone as calm as possible. Identify injured persons and apply first aid until help arrives. Again, it is most important to remain calm and reassuring. You will be grateful if you have had a course in first aid and CPR and even more so if your driver is qualified. And aren't you glad that you have the medical information from the passenger data sheets? Check it out for each injured person.

Illness

When a tour member becomes ill, the same procedure should follow. If it occurs in a public place you should try to get medical help as soon as possible. Ask the bus driver or a responsible tour member to summon the emergency service immediately. Stay with the patient until the doctor or ambulance arrives. If there is a traveling companion, he/she should accompany the patient to the hospital or clinic. If not, ask for a volunteer. Locate the patient's health insurance card and be sure to get the name of the medical personnel and hospital to which they will be going.

At this point, you need to stay with your tour group until you and the driver can plan an alternative activity for the next few hours. Perhaps it will be a return to the motel or a few hours at a nearby shopping mall.

Be glad that you studied the maps carefully so you know some of the resources of the area. Always establish a time to regroup, preferably in no more than two hours. Then, when you get your group back together you can update them on the situation and next steps.

That two hours will give you time to alert any of your suppliers about your emergency and delay. Then you can go to the hospital or clinic and get the necessary information from the attending physician. If a hospital stay will be necessary, telephone the family or contact person to arrange for their arrival and handling of the situation.

When you are sure that appropriate care is being given to the patient you can return to your group. Explain the circumstances factually and seriously, but as unemotionally as possible. You need to show that you care, but a dramatic summary will only unnerve your tour members more. Remember that they have witnessed a crisis and spent several hours of uncertainty about the outcome. Deep in each of their minds is the unsettling possibility that someday such a thing could happen to them. You need to speak of it as a rare, unexpected occurrence which calls on all of us to accept, adapt as necessary, and take it in stride. Recognize them for their stability and cooperation in the incident. Express gratitude that results weren't worse and credit them for helping make the most of a tough situation.

Resume your scheduled activities as soon as you can or innovate an impromptu activity for the evening. This is not a time for sitting in worried little groups, discussing the crisis. If the patient can quickly and comfortably return to the tour group, help him/her to do so with composure but do not delay your itinerary unnecessarily. If the patient is still hospitalized you can telephone daily to check up on his/her progress. Always report current information to the tour group.

You need to speak of an emergency as a rare, unexpected occurrence.

Liability

Throughout any emergency you need to keep a record of all services and persons involved.

Throughout any emergency you need to keep a record of all services and persons involved. Surely, that is the last thing you would naturally remember to do, but on a tour, your responsibilities are different. You will discover that each emergency carries with it a possibility of liability. In a large percentage of the cases, no charges are pressed. But you will be prepared with adequate data just in case. So accumulate the necessary information.

At the end of a tour when there has been an emergency, it is a good idea to fill out an injury/illness report (see Appendix #27). If the crisis occurred as a result of neglect on the part of any supplier, you can be certain that they were also concerned and have filed a report of the incident. However, if no supplier was involved and the responsibility seems to have been related to your management procedure, you may be wise to contact your attorney with your accident/illness report and data and a copy of your disclaimer statement.

Actually, there are not many parts of a tour when participants are not being served by one supplier or another so many tour managers feel fairly safe in functioning without liability insurance for their company. Other independent tour operators like the arrangement of working in affiliation with a local agency since they can arrange the protection of the liability insurance of the agency. But if you are functioning entirely on your own, you should investigate a liability insurance policy for your company. All major insurance companies sell policies that cover a wide range of liabilities. You need to contact your local firms and decide which coverage will serve your needs to the best advantage. It is money well spent to protect yourself from possible litigation. In the last analysis, your best insurance against problems includes:

- selecting reputable suppliers
- careful planning to anticipate and avoid problem situations
- establishing and maintaining positive and supportive relationships with clients at all times

Keep records of the accident/illness incident on file with your tour records so it will be available if it is ever needed. In most cases, the matters are quickly and satisfactorily resolved and dismissed.

The ultimate disaster, dreadful as it may be, is the possibility of a tour member's death while he/she is on the tour. If you devote many years to the tour business, it is entirely possible that you could experience such an incident. Of course, it is more likely with older travelers and can occur without warning even in the best planned situations.

As the tour director, you will have some special responsibilities in this event so we should at least be aware of them. As with other illness emergencies, you should call for medical help or a rescue team. Again, it is best to clear the other tour members from the area. They usually realize the critical nature of the problem and cooperate well.

When death occurs, you will need to call the county coroner. He may call the family of the victim or ask you to do so. Refer to your passenger data sheet to get the name of the person to notify. Find out the name of the funeral director from the family member. You should then pass that information on to the coroner so he can arrange for the transfer of the body.

Meanwhile, you should retrieve the personal belongings of the victim and make an inventory of them. It's a good idea for you to do that with another person for liability protection. You can get them back to the family upon your return. Later in the day, it is kind to call the family and reassure them about the arrangements that the coroner made. They will appreciate your caring and concern.

> **Keep records of the accident/illness incident on file so it will be available if it is ever needed**

Tour directing is not always an easy task but it will be filled with new and different experiences.

If the passenger was traveling with a companion, that person may also plan to return home. You should help him/her make arrangements, get to the airport, or whatever is necessary. You might want to contact a minister or priest to console the companion or mate in those interim hours during their shock and grief. When you return home with the tour group, you should visit the family and express your condolences.

Your tour group has waited patiently throughout this traumatic day. It hasn't been easy for them either. Now you need to get back to them and resume the itinerary of the tour. It might be appropriate to have a brief period of remembrance with a few remarks, a meaningful poem, and a moment of silent prayer. After that, your challenge is to get the group into a new frame of mind and ready for new adventures and fun. Tour directing is not always an easy task but you do have to admit, it will be filled with new and different experiences.

Thankfully, emergencies are few and far between. When they do occur, we know how to handle them, and our tour groups are grateful that we can do it so well.

Questions For Further Study

1. What can travelers do if they lose their traveler's checks?

2. What should tour members do if they lose their wallets?

3. How can you help tour members who are feeling airsick or seasick?

4. What is the best way to protect yourself from law suits, when tour members are sick or injured?

SPECIAL CONCERNS FOR CUSTOM TOURS

One of the most fascinating aspects of this business is the wide variety of groups and their assortment of tour purposes. Each new client who contacts your firm for services has a unique proposal for destinations and activities. One week, you may be planning with a group of antiques collectors about a trip to locations where they can explore and possibly bargain for treasures in their field of interest. Another week you may be assisting a choral group as they set up a concert tour to perform in eight different cities.

Each of the client groups can very likely represent an area with which you are unfamiliar. You need to work closely with the group representative to learn any important factors that will influence your tour planning. By the same token, the group representative has no background in tour management and will need to know how to share in your procedures.

The antiques group leader is enthusiastic. She has always looked forward to an opportunity like this. In fact, she may be over-estimating how much interest the other members really have. Supportive social conversation often indicates interest, but it is not a very good barometer of the actual reserving participants. The leader needs to survey the group

Cooperative Planning

The group leader may be completely unaware of the realistic costs that are going to be involved.

and come to you with a list of all possible tentative signers with minimum/ maximum figures in order for you to begin planning and negotiating on their behalf. Remember, actual participating members must reach a given number (usually 20-24) before group discounts will be offered.

Don't rely on the leader's assurance that as the trip departure draws closer, more people will "catch the excitement" and finally decide to go along. Many leaders do not have the marketing and promotional skills to fill the tour to its capacity. Besides, they don't realize that with the weeks and months of lead time, deposit deadlines will have long since passed when those tentative participants finally make up their minds.

The group leader, with no background in tour services, may be completely unaware of the realistic costs that are going to be involved. Her mental picture of the tour price may be based on bargain air rates she heard about and an economy rate hotel. Her envisioned estimate of the total tour price is practically impossible. You will need to gently point out the hidden costs of transfers, baggage handling, taxes and tips. She may have neglected to consider any group meals or admissions, of which at least a few need to be included.

You certainly don't want to dampen their enthusiasm, but they do need to be aware of everything before you invest considerable time and effort. A good way to handle this task is to show them a model trip plan with all the items included at realistic prices. As the leader translates the model form into her group needs, she is in a better position to determine the acceptability of her proposed tour.

Special Needs Of Special Groups

Certain aspects of a custom trip require knowledge and contacts that only people in that profession have. What kinds of facilities do they plan to see…museums, galleries, auctions, heritage homes? You as a tour planner are out of your league so you have to rely on officers of the group to make the necessary arrangements. They need to telephone or write the appropriate contact person at each of their chosen attractions and get the necessary information:

- type of attraction, location, names of group reservationist
- days and hours available for attendance by groups
- charges if required, group rates if available
- confirmation procedures if necessary

You can make suggestions that will help the leader in her negotiations. With luck, she won't come back to you reporting *"They said they'd be glad to have us come anytime."* Insist on definite confirmed days and times so your itinerary can provide the smoothly operating segments it needs. Your only alternative is to allow the group frequent and extended "on your own" intervals, and hope that the participants will gain the benefits they seek.

By systematically following your own planning routine you can avoid omitted considerations. Hopefully, you have also helped them become better planners for future tours they schedule.

Other Examples

Let's think about other kinds of special arrangements they may need to be made by the group's manager.

Often, an organization that is performing in one or several locations must have special equipment. Sometimes they need specific facilities and even certain conditions. You, as tour director, can't possibly know what all of these detailed needs are but the success of the tour and the cost of the trip are going to depend heavily on the tour manager's function. You may need to arrange for:

- locker/dressing rooms and shower facilities for sports groups

- transportation for equipment, musical instruments, costumes, athletic supplies, sound amplifiers
- rehearsal or practice facilities
- costuming rooms, staging, lighting, and sound facilities for performances
- risers, podium, a tuned piano or organ, a public address system
- special janitorial services

These are just a few of the multitude of details that the manager of the group must plan. All of those services involve timing and probably, extra charges. Up to now, these were the organization's problems but now the time and costs are affecting your itinerary, tour budget and even your liabilities regarding the tour.

More complexities arise when the appearances occur in several different cities. Some facilities charge extra fees (some require union personnel for certain services, some do not) and some do not allow organization staff members to take care of occasional details. You can easily understand that it is crucial to maintain excellent communication throughout the planning period.

Travel Study Tours

Educational institutions and agencies have continued to recognize the opportunities for learning that are available in travel experiences.

Hundreds of student groups are scheduled in field courses, both for academic credit and non-credit. There are a number of tour companies that specialize in planning and consulting for just these types of educational tours. Some are foreign exchange programs, research expeditions, and seminar/conferences. There are also several non-profit organizations that provide consultant services and package plans for educational groups.

Since many educational programs are planned for extended time intervals (a few weeks to even a year) they are usually organized as unescorted trips. The professor or subject matter specialist serves as the tour leader and actually supervises most of the tour. The tour companies function primarily as consultants, and may schedule and confirm transportation and lodging, at least. In many cases, a host is contracted in each major city or area to assist with the local procedures of the tour.

The academic leader of the group (class) has the responsibility for arranging the educational ingredients of the study tour. If it is a credit course, he/she follows the necessary preparations and procedures for it to become a recognized credit experience. Students enroll and pay registration fees as they do for any other course.

In order to be academically accredited, most course sequences involve pre-tour and post-tour sessions. The course materials and supplies, the professor's salary and courtesy fees for speakers and consultants are paid by the institution. The tour firm deals only with the costs of transportation, accommodations, transfers, and some meals in most travel-study tours.

On non-credit courses, the cost arrangements may be less clearly defined. However, these matters must be discussed in advance to avoid confusion in responsibility and authority regarding the operations.

Financial planning of travel study tours is particularly important because many students are on strained budgets. In tough economic times, most schools and colleges are also feeling the pinch and cutting on the frills for educational programs. As a consultant, you may be wise to search out economy services that are adequate for school groups. Consider dormitory facilities if available, student hostels, and sometimes a homestay program will fit in. Always be sure that such facilities are safe, clean, and conveniently located. By using homestay arrangements that are sponsored by international organizations, such as "People to People" you can be more assured that the situation is a safe one to include.

Questionable Situations

Economic stress may also cause tour sponsors and institutions to manipulate other profitable inclusions. Sometimes an enterprising tour leader will specify that the tour cost will include a free trip for a husband or wife who will be "helping to escort the tour." In a few weeks, you may discover that a teenage daughter and a mother-in-law are also eager participants if they can travel at half price. The fact remains that those charges will simply have to be absorbed into the students' tour price. This will not only be a hardship for the students, but may also limit the number who can afford to go.

When you are asked to serve as a consultant for a tour plan, you will discover that many group leaders never consider the expertise, time and effort that they are requesting. Ingenious discussions in a social situation suggest that you "take a look at our plans." As a professional consultant, you need to clarify whether they want you to be a consultant, and the fee that you will need to charge. Remember that you are accepting responsibility and liability in this role. By contracting your consulting service you will keep the arrangements on a business level. Be sure to define how much planning and negotiations they expect you to do and which they are certain they will carry out themselves.

Sometimes a school or college will channel their travel study courses through a special division of the institution. Here again you need to understand their policies and the arrangements they will carry out. That division may also see their role as a way to justify an additional charge for their services. On some occasions, they even use this opportunity to recoup the cost of the leader's salary or secretarial costs. After your diligent efforts to keep the students' tour price at an affordable level, this can defeat your entire purpose.

These are often personnel who are not skilled in tour management and marketing. They usually insist that they can easily handle the advertising and selling aspects of the tour. Their "promotional" efforts may be a routine announcement in the campus newspaper or a typed trip summary for a flyer which is distributed in classes. Obviously, these are not going to generate an enduring interest in the tour. You can provide the greatest help by offering practical, economical suggestions that will make their efforts more productive. Their ineffective, amateurish promotions reflect on your tour image and you don't need that.

There are many ways enterprising individuals use the benefits of group travel discounts for their own profits. Unfortunately, poor quality tours reflect on all of the tourism industry. Community social service agencies have been known to increase their prices on so called "nonprofit" trips for low income senior citizens so they can produce funds for their operational budgets. Always be aware of these practices and avoid involvement with them.

Our goal at all times is to provide a quality tour experience at a fair price in the safest and most professional conditions.

Questions For
Further Study

1. How are custom tours different from the general tour offerings?

2. What are the best ways for the group chairman and the tour director to divide responsibilities for the success of the tour?

CONCLUSION

When you fully understand a new career area and all that it has to offer, you can make your professional plans with confidence. By knowing the rewards and satisfactions you can tell whether you will be motivated enough to achieve them. Becoming aware of possible frustrations assures you that you know the whole scope of the tour management field. This manual was designed to help you do that.

Unlike many service industries, work in the tour business focuses on pleasure-oriented situations with people. Every special arrangement is planned to avoid problems and stress for you and your clients. When they are satisfied with their tour investment, it means that you can look forward to repeat business from them.

Now you realize that this career is filled with unlimited opportunities for the person who is serous about making a success of it. With the instructions and resources that are provided here, you can watch your program grow as you plan and market your tours. Experience is an excellent guide and each additional trip will give you more knowledge and confidence. You will also be pleased that you learn much from your contacts with other understanding professionals in the travel and hospitality industries.

Best wishes to you for a rewarding and profitable career in tour management.

APPENDIX

Airport _____

International ☐ Domestic ☐

Intrastate Airlines:

Airline _____ Phone _____

Direct Flights to Major Cities:

_____

_____

_____

_____

Airline _____ Phone _____

Direct Flights to Major Cities:

_____

_____

_____

_____

Airline _____ Phone

Direct Flights to Major Cities:

_____

_____

_____

_____

Commuter Carriers:

_____

_____

Commuter Carriers:

_____

_____

**Attach Schedules and
Other Relative Information**

City _____

Miles to _____ Time _____

Ground Transportation by:

    Supplier   Phone

_____ _____

_____ _____

_____ _____

Courtesy Transportation by Hotels:

_____

_____

_____

Parking: Short Term @$ _____ per hour

            Long Term @$ _____ per day

            Shuttle Service $_____

Terminal: # of Buildings _____

No. of Concourses _____ No. of Gates _____

Entrance Loading ☐ Yes ☐ No

Curbside Porterage ☐ Yes ☐ No

Administrative Offices _____

No. of Waiting Areas _____

Avg. Seating Each Area _____

Restroom Areas Each Level _____

Provisions for Handicapped _____

_____

Concessions _____

Auto Rental Suppliers   Phone #

_____

_____

Railroad Terminal _____

Intrastate Suppliers:

Amtrak (most domestic destinations)

Contact Name & Phone # for Group Travel:

_____

Direct Service To Major Cities:

_____

_____

_____

_____

_____

Group Reservation Procedures:

_____

_____

_____

Discount Policies:

_____

_____

_____

Payment Procedures:

_____

_____

_____

Cancellations/Penalties:

_____

_____

Location: _____

Terminal _____

Entrance Loading ☐ Yes ☐ No

Curbside Porterage ☐ Yes ☐ No

Check-in Area _____

_____

Waiting Area _____

_____

Seating for Groups _____

_____

Restroom Facilities _____

_____

Provisions for Handicapped _____

_____

Concessions _____

_____

Auto Rental Suppliers   phone #

_____

_____

Taxi, limo, bus service (for transfer)

_____

_____

_____

Parking: Short term @$ _____ per hour

        Long term @$ _____ per day

**Attach Current Schedules and
Note Availability of Food Service, and Other
Facilities on the Various Trains in Use.**

Use a separate sheet for recording information about each supplier. Minimum
requirements: air conditioning, comfortable reclining seats, clean lavatories,
large tinted windows, and a *functioning* public address system.

Motorcoach Company _____ Phone # _____

Group Reservation Contact _____

Address _____ City _____

Number of coaches in fleet? _____ Standard models _____ Capacity ea. _____

Deluxe models _____ Capacity ea. _____

Features	Standard	Deluxe
Drop Step for Easy Boarding		
Handrails at Entrance		
Overhead Racks for Carry-ons		
Tray-tables		
Radio/Stereo Equipment		
Televisions		
Wet Bar Facilities		

Drivers: Uniforms? _____ Professional Appearance, Attitude, Language _____

Safety / Maintenance Procedures During the Tour _____

Reservation Procedure: Contracted Price For Tour _____

Deposit Required? _____ Refundable? _____ Full Payment Due _____

Policies: Payment for Driver Lodging & Meals? _____

Gratuities for Drivers? _____

Liability Regarding Accidents, Injuries & Damage? _____

Cancellations _____

Penalities_____

By comparing the companies' rates, per mile, per day, per bid, you will be able to determine the best
service for the cost.

I.　**Background information**
　　When and where was the business organized?
　　What will be the basic structure—independent, partnership or agency affiliate?
　　Who will be the persons with authority for making decisions?

II.　**Description of the tour business you are planning**
　　What types of tours will you offer? What size and types of groups will you serve?
　　How many tours per season/year do you plan to operate? First year? Second and third
　　years? Five years? How much profit do you plan to realize at each stage? What factors
　　will help you most in your operations? What problems will you need to work around?

III.　**Survey of all of the suppliers to be used for your tours**
　　Which transportation services are available to you? What is the quality of service for
　　each? What are the best destination choices available for tours? What type of accom-
　　modations will you require for lodgings?

IV.　**Planning to be done for each season's tour series**
　　How will you set tour schedules, promotion and reservation deadlines? How much can
　　you afford to vary these schedules? How will you decide which tours are worth
　　repeating?

V.　**Pricing and profit system for your tour service**
　　What basis will you use for total price on each tour? What is the minimum profit
　　margin to expect? At what level will tours need to be canceled?

VI.　**Marketing procedures**
　　What methods of promotion will you use? How much of the tour cost will be used for
　　promotion? How will you decide which kind of advertising works best?

VII.　**Financial management and reporting**
　　What system will be used for financial records? How often will you evaluate the
　　system for needed improvements? How will you arrange for an annual audit? What
　　method will you use to accumulate tax information/records? Will you use a tax
　　consultant for annual reporting? How will you handle liability situations, if any?

Writing a plan will help you establish your operating policies. It is valuable for reference
when you need to consult with auditors, bankers and other professionals. Later, when you seek
ASTOA accreditation, you will have all of your business policies at hand.

As a tour director, you will be mainly interested in general maps of states and regions (road maps). But, for the details of itineraries, you will use special local maps of the city or area that you will be visiting. These will show you access routes to transportation terminals, hotels and various attractions. All maps include street names. Often, the numbering system for street addresses is indicated in the margin of a city map. These are a great help in locating a specific street address.

All maps are shown in scale, which is an accurate fraction of the actual distance. (For example, you will see ──────10────── showing that 1 inch equals 10 miles.) Sometimes they also list the distance in kilometers. Many maps include a mileage table which indicates the distance between any two major cities in that state.

On each map, you will find a legend, which lists the symbols that are used to provide information instead of words. Some of the symbols are in special colors. Learn to use them for convenient map use.

━━━━━━	Free Limited-Access Highways
━ ━ ━	Under Construction
══════	Toll Limited-Access Highways
════ ═:	Under Construction
────────	Other Four-Lane Divided Highways
════════	Principal Highways
────────	Other Through Highways
────────	Other Roads (conditions vary—local inquiry suggested)
━━ ━	Unpaved Roads (conditions vary—local inquiry suggested)
─ ─ ─	Scenic Routes
⬭	Interstate Highways
⬭	U.S. Highways
○⊂⊃	State and Provincial Highways
▢▢	Secondary State, Provincial and County Highways
◈	Interchange Ramp
▦	Golf Courses
▨	Parks (large)
▲▲	Parks (small)
⟩ *ENTR*	Park Entrances
✝	Cemeteries
▮	High Schools, Colleges
✚	Hospitals
▲	Shopping Centers
✠	Airports

Destination: (City, Region, Country) _____

Access Information:

    AIRPORT _____ miles

    Transfers to Location by ☐ Taxi ☐ Bus ☐ Other _____ Cost _____

    GROUND TRANSPORTATION: ☐ Train ☐ Bus

    Locations of Terminals: _____

    Transfers Available _____ Cost _____

Major Hotels: (Central Locations)   Group Price/Rm.

_____   _____

_____   _____

_____   _____

Major Hotels: (Suburban Locations)   Group Price/Rm.

_____   _____

_____   _____

Restaurants: (Well Located, Good Quality, Well Priced)

_____

_____

Special or Ethnic Restaurants: _____

Attractions: (Note Accessibility & Location)   Admission $

_____   _____

_____   _____

_____   _____

Shopping: (Unique Items, Special to the Area) _____

_____

Miscellaneous: (Safety on Streets, Accessible Beaches, Sports Facilities & Seasonal Events)

_____

_____

Name of Hotel: _____ ☐ Chain ☐ Independent

Address/State/Zip: _____

Phone (Local #) _____ 800 # _____

Number of Rooms & Rates

Standard (Single) _____ @ _____ (Double) _____ @ _____

Deluxe (Single) _____ @ _____ (Double) _____ @ _____

In-room Features: _____

_____

Non-smoking Rooms Available? .. ☐ Yes ☐ No

Handicapped Equipped Rooms? .. ☐ Yes ☐ No

Room Service? .... ☐ Yes ☐ No

Smoke Alarms Installed? .... ☐ Yes ☐ No

Sprinkler System? .... ☐ Yes ☐ No

Hotel Features:

Restaurants _____

Lounges _____

Shops _____

Pool (Health Facilities) _____

Courtesy Van Available _____

Parking Facilities _____

Baggage Handling   Curbside _____ Fee: _____

                                   To/From Rooms _____ Fee: _____

General Conditions:

Cleanliness _____ Courtesy _____

Decor _____ Maintenance _____

Tour # _____ **Destination** _____ **Date(s)** _____

SUPPLIER: _____   Contact Person: _____

Address/City/Zip _____   Phone _____

Deposit _____ due _____   Full pmt. _____ due _____

Date: _____   Contact: _____

Memo: _____

_____

_____

_____

_____

SUPPLIER: _____   Contact Person: _____

Address/City/Zip _____   Phone _____

Deposit _____ due _____   Full pmt. _____ due _____

Date: _____   Contact: _____

Memo: _____

_____

_____

_____

_____

SUPPLIER: _____   Contact Person: _____

Address/City/Zip _____   Phone _____

Deposit _____ due _____   Full pmt. _____ due _____

Date: _____   Contact: _____

Memo: _____

_____

_____

_____

_____

Rooming List *Appendix 9*

Tour: _____   Tour #: _____

Hotel: _____   Dates: _____

		SG	DBL

Name: _____   Name: _____ ☐ ☐
Street: _____   Street: _____
City/State/Zip: _____   City/State/Zip: _____

Name: _____   Name: _____ ☐ ☐
Street: _____   Street: _____
City/State/Zip: _____   City/State/Zip: _____

Name: _____   Name: _____ ☐ ☐
Street: _____   Street: _____
City/State/Zip: _____   City/State/Zip: _____

Name: _____   Name: _____ ☐ ☐
Street: _____   Street: _____
City/State/Zip: _____   City/State/Zip: _____

Name: _____   Name: _____ ☐ ☐
Street: _____   Street: _____
City/State/Zip: _____   City/State/Zip: _____

Name: _____   Name: _____ ☐ ☐
Street: _____   Street: _____
City/State/Zip: _____   City/State/Zip: _____

Name: _____   Name: _____ ☐ ☐
Street: _____   Street: _____
City/State/Zip: _____   City/State/Zip: _____

Name: _____   Name: _____ ☐ ☐
Street: _____   Street: _____
City/State/Zip: _____   City/State/Zip: _____

Name: _____   Name: _____ ☐ ☐
Street: _____   Street: _____
City/State/Zip: _____   City/State/Zip: _____

Name: _____   Name: _____ ☐ ☐
Street: _____   Street: _____
City/State/Zip: _____   City/State/Zip: _____

Tour #: _____   Tour _____   Date _____

Passengers _____   Tour Price _____   **Total Receipts** _____

Transportation Supplier _____

_____ miles _____ hours

Total Charges: _____

Accommodations Supplier _____

Number of Nights _____

_____ rooms _____ doubles @ _____

_____ singles @ _____

Baggage Handling _____

Total Charges: _____

Meal Supplier _____

Served: _____ Bkfst _____ L _____ Dnr _____ Snk

Total Charges: _____

Supplier _____

Served: _____ Bkfst _____ L _____ Dnr _____ Snk

Total Charges: _____

Supplier _____

Served: _____ Bkfst _____ L _____ Dnr _____ Snk

Total Charges: _____

Attractions Supplier _____

Number of Admissions _____ @ _____

Total Charges: _____

Miscellaneous Charges:

_____ @ _____

_____ @ _____

_____ @ _____

Total Charges: _____

GRAND TOTAL: _____   _____

BALANCE

Income Ledger *Appendix 11*

This is a record of all payments received. Since you may be accepting checks for more than one tour at one period, you must designate the tour number for each payment.

Date	Received from	Amt.	Chk/ Cash	Tour No.	Memo	Deposit Date

Always record payments received immediately, and before you deposit them in the bank. Be sure to indicate if the payment was for another person (as for a husband and wife). You will need each name later, as it appears on the passenger list. Check your income ledger each month when your bank statement arrives.

This record will list all money that is paid out of your business account. It is generally a good plan to set up a separate account at your bank and reserve it for business transactions only. If you take money out of that accunt, write a "cash" check to yourself, but do not pay personal bills from that account. It will be easier if you pay for everything by check. Casual petty cash payments are easily lost in the shuffle.

Date	Chk. No.	Payee	Amt.	Memo	Tour No.

Check this ledger against your bank statement every month. Be aware that your bank balance and tour profits may not seem consistent but at the end of the year the balances and profits should balance. Keeping these up to date will simplify your tax returns and help you plan for the future.

Use the plastic pin-on type of name tags. Professional appearing tags are easy to make and can be reused tour after tour. Ask your print shop to cut card inserts and print them with the name of your company. Type a list of your passengers and enlarge it on the copier. Snip the names apart and tape them onto the blanks. From your numbered passenger list, put the corresponding number in the corner of the name tag. This is the person's identification number for checking on or off the group activity.

Devise a method for passing out name tags in a simple routine. Use a mat or board about 12" x 15" for space where name tags can be arranged alphabetically. No fumbling through a packet or box to find the right one.

Collect the tags at the end of the tour. By replacing the insert name card, you can use the same set of plastic pin-on holders repeatedly.

22

Betty Roberts

ABC TRAVEL

Create your own convenient method to simplify the boarding—deboarding procedure. Here is a suggested system:

On an erasable surface, print the numbers 1-40 (or the total number of persons on the tour) with a permanent marker. On the back, tape a passenger list with the numbers used on the name tags (see page 194). While boarding, each passenger calls out the number on his/her name tag so you can cross it off the list with an erasable marker. When all numbers are checked, the group is ready to depart. One number left? Find out who is missing by checking the passenger list.

1 2 3 4 5 6 7 8
9 10 11 12 13 14 15 16 17
18 19 20 21 22 23 24 25 26
27 28 29 30 31 32 33 34 35
36 37 38 39 40

Erase the slash marks when finished and your permanent numbers remain, ready for your next check-in. A dry-erase board is ideal for this system.

Please fill in this page and return it to us. Thank you! Use a separate sheet for each person.

Name _____

Address _____ City _____ Zip _____

Telephone (Home) _____ (Business)_____

Occupation (Past or Present) _____

Special Interests & Hobbies _____

_____

_____

Please note any special celebrations or events while on this tour (birthday, anniversary, etc) _____

_____

_____

IN CASE OF EMERGENCY PLEASE NOTIFY

Name _____

Address _____ City _____ Zip _____

Telephone (Home) _____ (Business)_____

Name of Doctor _____

Address _____ City _____ Zip _____

Telephone _____

List any medications that you will be taking during this tour: _____

_____

_____

List any health conditions we should be aware of (heart condition, high blood pressure, diabetes, etc.)

_____

_____

GET ACQUAINTED CARD

This brief form is useful for short trips and excursions. Make it index card size and it will be perfect for filing in your customer file.

Name _____

Address _____ City _____ Zip _____

Telephone (Home) _____ (Business)_____

Occupation (Past or Present) _____

I am interest in ☐ 1 day trips ☐ 2 or 3 day trips ☐ longer trips

COURTESY NOTE FORM

Occasionally, a tour member opts to omit some segment of the itinerary to pursue another activity. Use this form so you have a record of their plan.

If you plan an activity which is not part of the set itinerary, please complete this form and return it to your tour leader to avoid unnecessary waiting and confusion.

Name_____

I will not be attending the following activity _____

_____

Instead, I plan to _____

_____

I will rejoin the group (list time and place) _____

_____

I accept full responsibility for myself while away from the tour group.

Signature _____

On most tours, you will want to rely on goodies that are inexpensive, tasty and nutritious. It is easy to take along a small package of cello-wrapped candies or nibblers. On an extended trip, you may prefer sweets since they are not as likely to produce thirst. Whatever you serve, be sure that it is fresh and good quality. Here are some time-tested examples:

- Individually wrapped candies
- Individually wrapped cookies
- Donut holes
- A small plastic baggie of fresh grapes (washed)
- A small packet of sweet cherries (washed)

Note

- Be sure to have paper napkins on hand for them, too.
- Remember to take along a bag for accumulating litter.
- Passengers are always delighted and impressed with a fresh, homemade cookie. For the price of a box of cookie mix and 45 minutes of effort, you can easily bake them the day before and they'll be ready. Purchased bakery cookies will cost about 5 times as much.
- Choose candies and cookies without nuts, caramel or crumbly surfaces.

Drinks on board are often a problem. The danger of spilled hot coffee is not worth the effort. Instead, serve it at a rest stop where each one can handle his own drink without problem. One good on-board possibility is the small cardboard cartons of unsweetened fruit juice with the handy straw attached. Put them in your freezer the night before so by the time you serve them they'll be thawed.

If an on-board lunch is necessary it is best to plan a brown bag meal. You can have them caterer prepared, but it is considerably more costly. Your best choices will be ham/cheese sandwiches (in plastic bags), a small bag of potato or taco chips, celery and carrot sticks, cookies or fruit. It is easier to serve at a rest stop when the beverage is no problem. If you prepare the brown bag lunches yourself, it will cost about 1/4 the price of the caterer's service so while you are watching profit margins, you may want to consider that.

On multi-day tours, your breakfast restaurant will usually fill your coffee thermos for a nominal fee. On occasions where lunch time will find you at a place away from food service, the breakfast restaurant may be willing to pack lunches for the group to carry along. Plan with them to include only foods that will not deteriorate with heat and motion. Transport perishable food in a cooler bin with liquid filled freezer blocks to maintain temperature, especially in warm weather.

If you find that you are preparing or handling food (beyond the snack or treat level) you may be wise to obtain a food handler's certificate. They are easy to get from your local Department of Health. Better to be on the safe side.

As you start out with your group on an extended trip, announce this game. The interest continues throughout the tour.

The driver has just recorded our starting mileage. On a piece of paper (you supplied) write down your guess as to how many miles we will have driven when we return. The guess that is the closest will receive a "fantabulous" prize.

Be sure the name is on each entry as you collect them. Hold the entries until you are about 20 miles from home. Get the driver's figures and award the prize.

A good choice for a prize:
    A bottle of wine from the winery you visited
    A small craft item from a gift shop you were in

They will enjoy and cherish the prize and your travelers will remember your fun-loving generosity. A good investment!

Playing Card Bingo

Abandon that Bingo set with so many pieces to lose and retrieve. Instead, use 4 decks of playing cards shuffled together. Deal 5 cards to each person. Instruct them that from your master deck of well-shuffled cards you will read off numbers. Use the microphone, speak slowly, and repeat each call "9 of spades... 9 of spades"

When a player has that card in his hand, he drops it to his lap. When you have called all five of his cards, he announces "BINGO!" and wins. This game moves quickly, so you could play five or six hands before the interest wanes. You could provide token prizes or even collect a nickel from each player each game. Accumulating the amount as a prize for the winner keeps it interesting.

Crossword Puzzle Appendix 18

Travel broadens your mind (and sometimes your waist line). As you wander, you will surely see wonders. The places below are famous for scenery, structures, gastronomical delights, history, entertainment and industry. Fill in the puzzle. Hints are listed on the next page to help you.

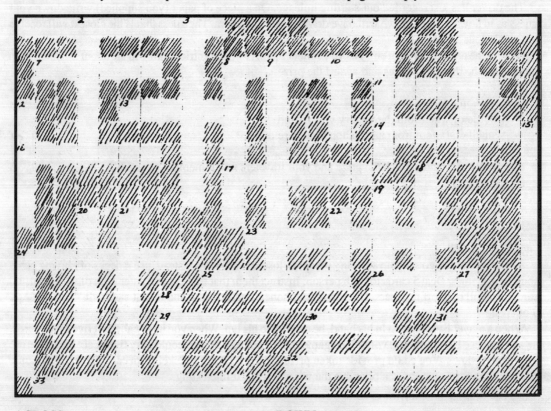

ACROSS		DOWN	
1. Bourbon Street	24. A Tree Grows	2. Disneyworld	20. Mythological Bird
4. Art Colony	25. Windy City	3. Opry Land	21. Glen Campbell's City
6. When in _ _ _ _	26. Witch Way	5. Boeing's Home	22. Gateway to Gold
7. Big D	29. Easily Tired	6. Stallone's Mts.	24. Old North Church
8. Parade of Roses	30. Desert Resort	8. City of Roses	27. Seasoned Saint
11. Menninger Clinic	31. Bay Place Color	9. Leave Your Heart	28. Not Wells
13. Mile High City	32. Virginia Mts.	10. A Great Lake	30. Resort City
14. Show Place	33. Red Stick	12. Friendly Ghost	
16. Gateway Arch		15. Oldest Settlement	
17. Disneyland		18. Abe's Namesake	
23. Small Boulder		19. Black Hills Four	

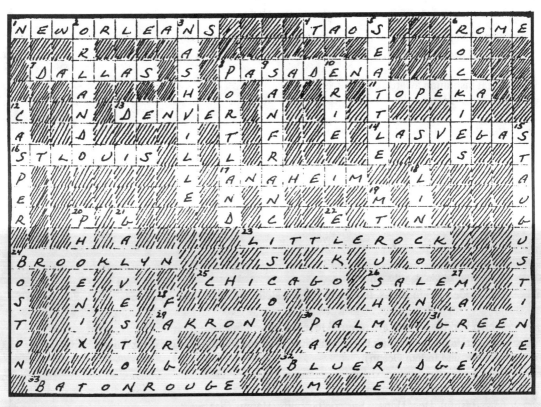

HINTS

Akron (OH)

Anaheim (CA)

Baton Rouge (LA)

Blue Ridge Mts (VA)

Boston (MA)

Brooklyn (NY)

Casper (WY)

Chicago (IL)

Dallas (TX)

Denver (CO)

Elko (NV)

Erie (PA)

Fargo (ND)

Galveston (TX)

Green Bay (WI)

Las Vegas (NV)

Lincoln (NE)

Little Rock (AR)

Mt. Rushmore (SD)

Nashville (TN)

New Orleans (LA)

Orlando (FL)

Palm Beach (FL)

Palm Springs (CA)

Pasadena (CA)

Phoenix (AZ)

Portland (OR)

Rockies

Rome (NY)

St. Augustine (FL)

St. Louis (MO)

Salem (MA)

San Francisco (CA)

Sault Ste. Marie (MI)

Seattle (WA)

Taos (NM)

Topeka (KS)

Here are some examples of simple quiz games that you might use to melt the miles and shorten the travel time. (Answers included)

Trivia

- Name the man who, with his son, carved the faces on Mt. Rushmore.
  (ans. Gutzom Borghum)

- What institution awards the Pulitzer prizes?
  (Columbia University)

- Prohibition became law by the 18th amendment of the constitution.
  What amendment repealed it? *(ans. 21st)*

- What does VHF on your television dial stand for?
  (ans. very high frequency)

Game of Sevens

- Name the seven deadly sins.
  (ans. pride, covetousness, lust, envy, anger, sloth, and gluttony)

- Which bodies of water are referred to as the Seven Seas?
  (ans. Arctic Ocean, Antarctic Ocean, North Pacific, South Pacific, North Atlantic, South Atlantic, and Indian Ocean)

- Name Snow White's Seven Dwarfs.
  (ans. Bashful, Doc, Dopey, Sneezy, Grumpy, Happy, Sleepy)

- The Declaration of Independence began with seven famous words. What are they?
  (ans. "When, in the course of human events")

- If you cited *"We hold these truths to be self evident. . ."* that was the second paragraph of the Constitution. If you said, *"We the people of the Untied States. . ."* that was the preamble to the Constitution, don't feel bad, You're in a big club!

Forget about group singing! Try these musical games instead.

Memory Game

On the way to a musical comedy production, ask group members to list all of the songs they can remember from that album. (For example: Sound of Music) Have them sign their names to their sheets before you collect them and after the performance, check the lists. The most correct items on the list identifies the winner.

Twelve Days of Christmas

Coming into the holiday season, here is a fun activity. Ask tour members to list the number of the items for each of the Twelve Days of Christmas. Award a prize for the list that is most correct.

Name That Tune

On a blank audio tape, record 6 note beginnings of 10 familiar songs. Play the tape, allowing two minute intervals between songs, so they can write down the titles. Award a prize for the most correct list.

Familiar Tunes

Select an old familiar song and ask seat partners to work together to write all of the words to the first verse.

Example—PUFF, THE MAGIC DRAGON or
HOW MUCH IS THAT DOGGIE IN THE WINDOW

Again the pair that get their verse right first wins.

On numerous occasions, you will need to have small items to use as prizes for games and activities. Inexpensive little tokens serve this purpose well so watch for clever ideas at 10¢ to $1 and keep them on hand for those times when you'll need them. Choose items that are small, useful, and appropriate to the age group. Here are a few examples:

- A lottery ticket
- A small decorative magnet
- Colorful memo pads
- Ball point pens
- Pen lite flashlight

- Rain scarf or bonnet
- Fabric Carry-on bag
- Tiny stick-on digital clock
- Clever key ring
- Photo insert for a wallet

If you have a Polaroid camera, a fun activity is to take the winner's picture and give it to him/her to keep. Some of the above listed items are available from promotion/advertising companies in quantity. You could be sure to carry the name of your tour company on the prize so then it becomes a smart bit of advertising as well.

Use this space for other fun ideas to remember:

Here are a few examples of humor that are appropriate for your group.

The teacher wrote on the chalkboard, "I ain't had no fun this summer at all." Then she asked a youngster in her class, "Susan, what would you suggest that I do to correct that statement?" Susan studied the sentence for a moment and replied, "Get another boyfriend!

....

A mother tried to awaken her 6year-old son so he could get on his way to school. Finally he half-opened his eyes, looked at her with disgust and remarked, "Whoever invented morning sure made it too early."

....

Minister: "If there is anyone here who knows of a truly perfect person, please stand up."
After a long pause a meek looking fellow in the back stood. "Do you really know a perfect person?" he was asked.
"Yes, sir I do," answered the little man.
"Would you please tell the congregation who this rare, perfect person is?" pursued the preacher.
"Yes, sir, my wife's first husband."

....

Three girls were talking about the kind of man they wanted to marry.
Wilma: "I want to marry a food-market owner so I can get our food for nothing."
Jan: "I want to marry a dress-shop owner so I can be well dressed for nothing."
Ellen: "I want to marry a preacher so I can be good for nothing."

....

For an amusing treat, fill pill bottles (available from your drug store) with colored jelly bellies. Paste on the following label.

> Older Folks Pills
> Baldness: White   Deafness: Orange
> Constipation: Green   Wrinkles: Pink
> Senility: Black   Hardening of the arteries: Red
> Impotency: Better try one of each

Jokes are taken from Pocket Smiles by Robert C. Savage Tyndale House Publishers, Inc. Wheaton, Illinois

Heavenly Father, look down on your humble tourist who travels this earth mailing postcards, walking around in drip-dry underwear, carrying armfuls of souvenirs.

We beseech you that our plane be on time, that we receive our very own luggage at each stop, that our overweight luggage go unnoticed, and that the customs officials be always understanding.

We pray that the phones work, the operators speak our tongue, and that there is no mail waiting from home causing us to cancel the rest of our trip.

Lead us to good inexpensive restaurants, where the wine is included in the price of the meal and the coffee is not too strong to drink.

Give us strength to visit museums and cathedrals, but if we skip historic monuments to take a nap after lunch, have mercy on us for our flesh is weak.

Protect our wives from bargains they cannot afford. Lead them not into temptation for they know not what they do or buy.

Keep our husbands from looking at foreign women and comparing them to us. Save our husbands from making fools of themselves in nightclubs and please do not forgive them their trespasses for they know exactly what they do.

And when the tour is over, grant us the favor of finding someone who will look at our videotapes and listen to our stories. We ask in the name of American Express, Sheraton, Hilton Hotels and the government of the land.

Amen!

~Source unknown

As a tour director or escort, you need to plan for your own personal convenience and comfort during the tour. Remember to:
- Start each tour as rested as possible.
- Leave copies of tour information in your workplace in case of an emergency.
- Arrange for a person who can take care of urgent matters at home base.

Professional appearance:
- Be well groomed with business-like apparel. Always wear your permanent tour director's badge.
- Choose an appearance that makes you readily identifiable in a crowd. You don't need a uniform, but you can select a certain color to wear, consistently throughout the tour.
- Limit the number of outfits, by versatile changes, with shirts, blouses, scarves, etc.
- Include a sweater or vest for extra cool days.
- Take an all weather topcoat, rainhat and umbrella.
- Use small, secure containers for cosmetics.

Handy to have along:
- Zip closure bags for soiled or damp clothes
- A simple four-function calculator
- The remote device for your telephone answering machine
- A spot lifter in a secure container
- Tissues, wet wipes, safety pins
- A purse sized flashlight
- Secure money containers (both personal and business)
- A small pair of scissors, a bottle opener and a corkscrew

In your briefcase: (keep it with you at all times)
- Your tour folder, with itinerary, passenger lists
- Personal data sheets, rooming lists
- Confirmation data for each supplier
- Checks for balance payments, unsigned until payment
- Packages of tickets that are pre-issued
- Maps, both general and for specific areas
- Paper and pencils for the group members

Your first aid kit does not need to be large or bulky, but it should have an assortment of clean fresh supplies. Many buses have their own kits but you're never sure how adequate they are. Here are some of the items you will want to include:

- Aspirin (or one of the substitutes)
- Pepto-Bismol or Immodium (for diarrhea or stomach upsets)
- Dramamine (or other motion sickness remedy)
- An antibiotic ointment (for scrapes or cuts)
- A hydracortisone cream (for stings, bites and sunburn)
- A small tube of Vaseline
- A small bottle of anti-bacterial soap
- Smelling salts
- Artificial tears and an eye cup
- A small bottle of spot remover
- Denture adhesive and dental cleanser
- Band-Aids (assorted sizes) and tape
- Q-Tips and gauze

RULE: Do not provide any medication or prescription substances.

Your responsibility is only to relieve pain and prevent infection. Beyond that, the patient should be treated by medical personnel. It is advisable to make the kit available to the passenger so they can select the remedy or treatment they prefer. Then, you would not be liable for deciding on treatment with negative results.

Clothes

Women's Blouses and sweaters

US	6	8	10	12	14	16	18
UK	28	30	32	34	36	38	40
Europe	36	38	40	42	44	46	48

Women's Dresses, Suits and Coats

US	4	6	8	10	12	14	16
UK	6	8	10	12	14	16	18
Europe	34	36	38	40	42	44	46

Women's Shoes

US	4	5	6	7	8	9	10
UK	2l/2	3t/2	4-1/2	5l/2	6l/2	7l/2	8l/2
Europe	35	36	37	38	39	40	41

Men's Shirts

US	14	14-1/2	15	15-1/2	16	16-1/2	17
Europe	36	37	38	39	40	41	43

Men's Suits, Pants and Sweaters

US	34	36	38	40	42	44	46
	(S)	(M)	(M)	(L)	(XL)	(XL)	(XL)
Europe	44	46	48	50	52	54	56

Men's Shoes

US	7	8	9	10	11	12	13
UK	6	7	8	9	10	11	12
Europe	39-1/2	41	42	43	44-1/2	46	47

Kids

US	3	4	5	6	6X
UK	18	20	22	24	26
Europe	98	104	110	116	122

Weight Ounces to Grams

Oz (lb)	1	2	3	4	5	8	12	16
GM	28	57	85	113	142	227	340	454
GM (kg)	10	20	30	40	50	100	250	1000
Oz	0.35	0.7	1.05	1.4	1.75	3.5	8.8	35.4

Pounds to Kilograms (ton)

lb.	1	2	3	5	10	44	100	2240
Kg.	0.45	0.9	1.36	2.27	4.5	20	45	1016
Kg.	1	2	3	5	10	25	100	1000
lb.	2.2	4.4	6.6	11	22	55	220	2204

Driving - Miles to Kilometers

KM	1	5	10	20	30	40	50	100
Miles	0.6	3	6	12	18	25	31	62
Miles	1	5	10	20	30	40	50	100
KM	1.6	8	16	32	50	64	80	160

Liters to Gallons

Liter		1	3	5	10	25	100
Gallon (US)	0.27	0.82	1.4	2.8	6.9	28	
Gallon (UK)		0.22	0.66	1.1	2.2	5.5	22

Tire Pressure PSI -KG/CM$_2$

PSI	16	18	20	22	24	26	28	30
KG/CM$_2$	1.1	1.3	1.4	1.5	1.7	1.8	2.0	2.1

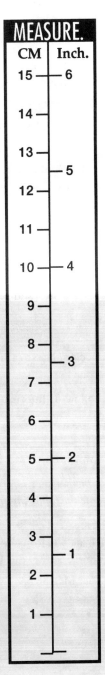

TEMP.

°F	°C
212	100
210	
200	90
190	
180	80
170	70
160	
150	60
140	
130	50
120	
110	40
100	37
90	30
80	20
70	
60	
50	10
40	0
30	
20	-10
10	
0	- 20

MEASURE.

CM	Inch.
15	6
14	
13	
12	5
11	
10	4
9	
8	3
7	
6	
5	2
4	
3	1
2	
1	

Injury/Illness Report *Appendix 27*

Tour Member's Name _____

Address _____ City _____ Zip _____

Tour Member's Insurance Co. _____

Policy Number _____

Type of injury or symptoms of illness _____

_____

_____

Circumstances of the problem _____

_____

_____

Date of injury or illness onset _____

Reported by _____ Date/Time _____

Medical attention arranged _____

_____

_____

Doctor / Nurse / Clinic _____

_____

Follow-up Information _____

_____

_____

_____

If the patient prefers no medical attention or treatment for the injury or illness, he/she should sign and date the following form.

Thank you for your concern about my injury/illness, but I feel that medical attention or treatment is unnecessary at this time.

Tour Member _____ Date _____ Hour _____

Tour # _____ Destination _____

Signature _____

Although the traveling public is increasingly aware of safety concerns, many people neglect their cautions when they travel with a group. Here are some warnings that may be helpful for tour leaders to share with their members. These are listed by Bob Burke, who is Director of Corporate Services and Safety at Monsanto, Inc.

"Travelers should always be on guard and if you feel something is wrong in a strange situation, it probably is, so get out of that situation. Avoid alcohol because drinking can lead to disorientation and set you up for problems. Take time to learn the layout of a city or neighborhood you are visiting." He offered the following suggestions:

- Travel with a buddy when possible.
- Don't wear fancy jewelry.
- Carry a purse over one shoulder, not across your chest or around your neck (it could cause injury in a purse-snatching attempt); don't wear high heels, and don't wear a tight dress (it restricts movement).
- Carry your wallet in a front pocket.
- Don't carry a lot of packages.
- Don't carry weapons or security noisemakers (they engender too much confidence).
- If attacked, go for the eyes or grab and crush the genital area (don't use your knees) and yell.
- Avoid automatic teller machines that are not in well-lighted areas and are not patrolled with a security camera.

At hotels, Burke suggested the following

- Put valuables in the hotel's safe.
- Never leave your room door ajar.
- Make sure your door closes properly and locks.
- Verify by phone any request by a staffer or repair person to visit your room.
- Be aware of the neighborhood in which the hotel is located before going outside.
- Keep a flashlight handy in case of a power outage.
- Carry a doorstop to stick under a locked door for added protection.
- Carry a boat horn or other portable alarm to keep next to your bed.
- Don't use a hotel's workout room unless it is kept locked or is staffed.
- If porter service is available to carry your bags to your room use it.
- Never open the door to your room to someone you don't know. Call the front desk if in doubt.
- On leaving the hotel, don't wear a meeting name tag.
- Don't carry fancy luggage.

At the airport

- Avoid "bandit" or "gypsy" cabs, which are unlicensed vehicles. Limousines and airport buses may be safer than cabs.
- Prearrange airport transfers with your hotel in a foreign country.
- Be aware that baggage theft is becoming increasingly common.
- Be aware that pickpockets often work in pairs.
- Don't put handbags or laptop computers on hooks in restrooms; thieves can grab them.

Travel Weekly, July 18, 1994, Expert Warns: Travel Safety Starts With You, by Fran Golden

GLOSSARY

- **Advertising:** Technique or materials used to promote sales

- **Affinity Tours:** A tour that is planned specifically for a group made up of members of an organization.

- **Attraction:** Sights, locations, events or presentations that a tour group visits.

- **Boarding Pass:** Section of an airline ticket which is presented at the gate in order to board a plane.

- **Carrier:** Any company that transports customers by land, air; or sea.

- **Carrousel:** A moving circular rack where luggage is placed for claim by passengers.

- **Charter:** An arrangement with a carrier to have the exclusive service of a vehicle for one specific group.

- **City Guide:** An escort who accompanies a tour group throughout a city tour and comments on the sights and locations enroute.

- **City Tour:** A sightseeing tour around a city during which a guide points out major highlights to passengers.

- **Check-in:** Procedure in which clients need to register and provide identification, to obtain the services a hotel, transportation or other facility.

- **Check-out:** Procedure when leaving a hotel or other facility, usually with the closing of payments for charges.

- **Client:** A customer who will buy a product or service.

- **Competitors:** More than one business offering similar or comparable services to the same clients.

- **Commissions:** A percentage of the sales price of an item or service. It is paid back to the tour company or travel agency.

- **Continental Breakfast:** A light breakfast meal, usually including juice, coffee and a roll. Often complimentary to hotel guests.

- **Corporate Rate:** A special rate of charges , arranged by a business and a supplier.

- **Cruise Director:** The person who serves as the main escort for a cruise ship and directs the social activities and events.

- **Customs:** The governmental agency that collects fees or taxes on items brought into the country. Also controls the entry of forbidden items.

- **Deposit:** A payment of money that is required in order to confirm a reservation.

- **Direct Flight:** A plane flight that reaches the destination without requiring passengers to change planes at any point.

- **Disclaimer:** Sometimes called a waiver - a printed statement by the tour operator declaring the limitations of responsibilities for the tour conditions.

- **Docent:** A guide at a museum or gallery, sometimes a volunteer.

- **Domestic Tour:** A tour within the borders of the country where the travelers reside.

- **Duty-free Shop:** A store where tourists who are leaving on international tours can buy items that have no tax or duty.

- **Excursion:** A trip that includes one or more destinations and returns to the starting location.

- **Express Airline:** An airline that provides extended flights to destinations that are not served by major airline schedules.

- **Familiarization Trip:** A trip arranged for travel personnel to become acquainted with the sites and services at a particular destination.

- **Fixed Costs:** Expenses of a tour that remain the same, regardless of the number of persons going on the tour.

- **Foreign Independent Tour (FIT):** A prepaid, unescorted trip that is arranged specifically for individuals or a few people.

- **Gate Area:** Area from which a tour group boards a plane or motorcoach.

- **Ground Operator:** A tour operator that provides services to other tour groups that come in from outside areas.

- **Group Rate:** A price offered by a supplier for services to a group of tour participants.

- **High Season:** the time of year when a particular destination is popular for tourists.

- **Inbound Tour Operator:** A tour company that specializes in arranging tours for groups from other countries.

- **Incentive Tour:** A group tour that is offered by a business firm as a reward to employees that have shown superior performance.

- **Intermodal Travel:** Trips that are arranged to use several types of transportation during the tour.

- **Itinerary:** A sequenced list of the group members' activities throughout each day of the tour.

- **Jet Lag:** A physical reaction that tourists often experience when crossing into other time zones. Normal body stability may be affected.

- **Low Season:** The time of year when a particular destination is not popular with most tourists.

- **Kickback :** A payment given to tour leader, for bringing a group into a shop, attraction or food service.

- **Marketing:** A process of planning, promoting and selling group tours.

- **Motorcoach tours:** A trip that is planned to transport group members to their destination and return primarily by the use of motorcoaches.

- **Non-commissionable**: Established price, with no percentage returned to the tour company or travel agency.

- **Non-stop Flight:** A plane trip that schedules no stops from departure to arrival at the destination.

- **No-show:** A person who does not use or cancel a reservation.

- **Outbound Tour Operator:** A tour company that takes passengers from one country to a destination in another country.

- **Outside Sales Person:** A representative of a tour company who solicits business for groups and receives a part of the commission as payment for each sale.

- **P.A. - Public Address System:** The microphone and speaker system for use in speaking to groups.

- **Package Tour:** A number of travel arrangements planned together for a client and sold at a single price.

- **Passport:** A document provided by the government for travelers so they may enter another country. It establishes their identity.

- **Porter:** The baggage handler at a terminal or hotel.

- **Rack Rate:** The established price that a hotel usually lists for its room prices.

- **Routine:** A sequence of procedures that a tour director follows on all of the tours.

- **Security Gate:** An entrance area in an airport concourse, where passengers are checked for illegal items, materials and weapons.

- **Shuttle:** Ground transportation between 2 or more terminals or facilities for the convenience of transfer of passengers.

- **Space:** The term given to seats or accommodations that are available for passengers on a tour.

- **Supplier:** A provider of travel services, such as, airlines, motorcoach firm or hotel.

- **Tour Director:** The person who manages the activities of a group throughout a tour. Also called tour manager, leader or escort.

- **Transfer:** To transport a traveler from a terminal or facility to the next location of activity.

- **Visa:** A permit obtained from a foreign government allowing a traveler to enter their country. Not required by some countries.

- **Voucher:** A coupon or order that can be used as payment for goods and services. Usually paid for in advance.

INDEX

E

F

G

I

L

M

N

O

P

R

S

T

U